Lessons

A diary for my daughter and a message to my son

Jason Allday

Copyright © 2020 Jason Allday
All rights reserved.
ISBN-13 9798584225483

Lessons from a Father to his children

A diary for my daughter and a message to my son

Doing the right thing.

Offering choices is easy: it is making the right choice that will always be hard. That has always been my dilemma, and never truer than when your integrity and morals are in question. More often than not, the easier option is to fold, to cave and take the easy way out. That is the everyday option we all face. A friend once told me he found himself in a situation where a gun was pointed at a close friend, he was given a very clear ultimatum by the gun-wielding villain. He had to make a decision, to follow the villain and move in a different direction in terms of his involvement the bit of illegal business or .... The called for the trafficking of counterfeit money. I understand the amount was just short of one hundred thousand pounds. Far from enough to buy a villa in the sun and call it a day, but all the same not pocket change, and certainly not worth a friends life. Had my friend decided to not to challenge the other villain he would've been a lot wealthier, but his friend would've been dead. My pal later said to me that your friends are worth more than any amount of money, and integrity had no price tag. What better way to exemplify your loyalty and integrity than when a person's life is a choice over money?

Most situations, they're far from tailor made or mapped out from a textbook that will prompt a perfect safe path. I was educated to believe we all had a choice when it came to the difference between right and wrong. In the case of illegal activity, there's a few standard beliefs that are of common understanding and form the basis of trust between fellow criminals. They were, 'never your own', 'you live by the sword and you die by the sword', 'loyalty unto death', 'never grass' and the list goes on but you get the picture. There are people, criminals, and ex criminals that claim this is 'old hat' and that they don't believe it was ever true, that there's 'no honour amongst thieves'. Those making this claim are the ones I steer clear of, and who typically have no morals or integrity, and they didn't to begin with. How can you place your trust someone that is not willing to subscribe to, or question a set of principles? These fence sitters, in my opinion, are the ones that from their initial involvement in crime, have entered the game with only their self-serving, and have selfish interests at heart and those that question the laws and rules, are the ones who are willing to break them, at your cost

A commonplace situation is the general public simply being in the wrong place at the wrong time, and more often than not, a clear example of this is a bank robbery. The stakes are high enough with the punishment and lengthy prison time hanging over any failed robbery, which may then prompt the criminal to question or push their principles aside, for those committing the crime to warrant someone's selfish best interest of escape, success or survival over a lump of porridge, they then cast aside the criminal code as it no longer serves their need. So what would the outcome be if an innocent bystander was simply drawing out a few quid from their local bank and before you could say, "everyone on the ground now!" when a team of hooded, armed to the teeth money getters come in to make an unauthorised withdrawal? It's inevitable that Joe public has now become part of the equation. This is makes the criminal code contradictory, the belief of 'never your own', but whose money is being stolen? I'm first person to favour a villain here, as contrary to public belief, the last thing a villain wants is to hurt Joe Public, they want to score from the greedy corporates and will look to exclude any public involvement. The discharging of shotguns, screaming, shouting and carelessly destroying property is just for the movies. Never has a plan been executed with the intention or thought of involving or harming Joe public, this would not benefit the money getters agenda. Villains seek at all times to avoid collateral damage or a delay in getting the job done, they are not on overtime, nor do they get a bonus for letting guns off, or making a racket. There are of course internal laws and rules dictating the well-being, safety and sanctuary of the general public, and I'm far from condoning any illegal acts or bad behaviour or violence against them; but then, I wasn't there to know the reasoning or justification behind the robbery either. Many villains I know don't have a 'welfare state' of mind or an option of looking to live off of government benefits. For them it's a matter of their integrity - they'd rather go hungry or commit armed robbery to get ahead, than ask for a hand out from the government. There is a difference between an able bodied person who's too lazy to get off his arse and get ahead than someone who's been dealt an unfair hand in life and is restricted in their abilities. Set a standard - For some that simply doesn't interpret all of life's options and possibilities, they simply go with what they know. If I were to use two very talented individuals as a comparison, it would be Elvis Presley and Smiley Louis. Smiley originally performed a song called 'One Night of Sin'. This is a heart wrenching, soul filling song. Depth, history and volume can be measured when you listen to both the music and vocals. It was later released on a much more commercial level by Elvis. The point being, if you're going to emulate or do something already done, make an effort worth giving credit to both you and your predecessor - failing that, be an original not a carbon copy of someone else.

Success is a matter of individual interpretation - It was said "I'd rather live one day as a lion than a lifetime as a lamb!" I'd even go as far to say Jimmy Cliff said it best, "I'd rather live as a free man in my grave than alive as a puppet or a slave". For many it means extra work; I personally don't see an 80-hour workweek as freedom! A close friend I have, who is an active member of the criminal world, said he holds the upmost respect for those that can do the 9-5 job, as no matter what enterprise he pursues in earning, it seems easier than the average Joe routine. Again, life isn't available in textbook form, with an index mapping out all its questions and answers. You have to do things for the right reasons and remember you will never have failed at anything until you give up; and if you make a mistake, that simply means that you are at least trying.

Be careful who you listen to. Politicians, I won't tarnish all with the same brush, as I'll only put a stain on my own overalls. I was asked why I relate to villains more than a politician? It's simple! Why should a person have to stand on a podium and shout to be heard? If a person has anything to say that is of value, then it should be spoken not screamed or repeated. I could pick up a phone and have a conversation with anyone of the people mentioned in here, but it would be a conversation that would give credit to their intelligence. Some of those put in public office you will notice during their public address and speeches will bang their fists, so as to give a deliverance with volume of speech and not content and if it's the icing on the cake you're looking for, they'll repeat themselves, as liars do, so as to convince themselves what they're saying is of value. When I'm told something that is of benefit I only have to be told it once. Business is war by another name, and villains are the government's biggest competitor. That's why I've always voted for the underdog.

Business is business and to go further criminals or villains could be considered more successful in many people's eyes than a legitimate government. In the business world, if you want to be successful you'll start by concentrating on your local community, as they're typically the most consistent buyer. A Japanese villain told me a philosophy he was once taught, that if you were to drop a pebble in a pool of water, the strongest ripples will be those closest to where the pebble dropped. A Villains success can be easily measured by his illegitimate gains, but a true villain is more successful by what could be referred to as his infrastructure. Every leader in history has only been successful because of his generals, captains and soldiers. In the world of villainy there aren't titles as such, but one, 'your own!' I can easily speak of London but I'm friends with villains from Birmingham to Scotland. Success for villains from different parts of the country exists for one simple reason. They hold the same manner of understanding and respect for the type of business they conduct. They don't airbrush, misconstrued or glamorise what they do. There's a very clear, cut and dry method and approach to how they do what they do. With regard to Scotland and the friends I have north of the border, I maintain one simple belief, that if you befriend a true Scotsman, then you have a friend for life.

Know your roots - Territorial imperative? Live life and have a standard of beliefs. I believe in a system that was best explained by a radio talk show host. I won't take credit for it but it's a system I support 100%. His motto is one that defines borders, language and culture; this will allow you to have an identity, know who you are and will uphold and promote the sovereignty of your nation. I have friends that are in many cases first generation English and it was the qualities that were installed within them whilst growing up in an English society that made them the men they are today. Their parents came to England and as in all of their stories, they wished not only for a better life but what was once clearly seen in England and that was a culture that took great pride in its political and cultural achievements. England, like most developed countries has many negatives, but in my opinion England's history and its positive achievements far outweighs its negatives. Acknowledge your mistakes and invest in your achievements. One thing I've always despised is the racial agitators and that is from any race; I see more gained in terms of pride and accomplishment when you get an individual who rose above all odds to make an iconic impression upon a culture and race. BB King is an exceptionally talented man, who even though being born in a shack in a Cotton field, being a diabetic and having the odds heavily stacked against him, managed to perform in just one year over 300 performances, and all the time not claiming one government hand out. That there to me is an inspiration and a credit to any working man.

Value - My friendships allowed me to be able to walk away from any conversation without a deficit with those I call friends. You should hold a positive and enriched relationship with those you call friends, as true friends are a rare commodity; a brother from another mother. Never ask for anything that can't be given in return. Simple principles. Dream-Nostalgia - be a thinker and a dreamer; this promotes a level of individualism in your identity and draw positives from your cultural past. Don't let your imagination be downplayed or derailed by those that are opposed to your individual thinking. The same liberal thinkers class those that are organised as someone suffering with OCD, when In fact it's simply a person with a level of discipline. That need to 'pigeon-hole' and label us limits free creative thinking.

Class - When I talk to friends that were very active in crime in the 60's & 70's, there was a standard of life that promoted a high level of personal pride in appearance, a smartness and class. A Woman was wined and dined. The villains were polished and classy, not just criminals, but also gentleman. There was without question violence but also a level of respect and discipline within the ranks. Say what you will, but personal standards have slipped in mainstream society today. There's more respect given for having a bigger TV than the courtesy extended to others in today's society. The pals I have will talk of Frank Sinatra and the Kray twins in the same manor of respect and tone; class, pure class. It was an era that today provokes nostalgia, for many an era that promoted class as experienced within and without the criminal world. A friend once told me it was commonplace back in the day to have a friend within power and sometimes government as it was within the underworld. More often than not, the two would have heard of each other and typically done business with each other; if not directly then through other associates. A mutual understanding and expectancy benefited two divided worlds only separated by mainstream media and public perception. If the truth was known, one was no more 'criminally' active than the other.

Stand for something or you'll fall for nothing - Who are you if you don't hold to your beliefs? I was once told that in life, you're either playing the role of the Shepherd or the sheep. Whatever role you fill, play the role and respect your position. Having direction aids your journey with course and motive. In fact all civilised walks of life wake up with a premeditated outset, or at least a plan of action. The bank robber and bank clerk know their jobs. The single mother struggling to make ends meet and an airline pilot know their objective and so can measure success; equally important roles, lives are dependent on their both. At least have a thought in your head that'll get you where you want to be and again beware of those oppressors who in a heartbeat want to quell or destroy your natural intelligence and survival instincts.

I'm not going to be a righteous indignant and claim any form of major achievement, other than I listen to those that hold both more or less experience on matters at hand. Always remember there's a difference in what you say and what you do. I don't have all the answers and I don't know anyone that does. For that you'd need a sage, not a simple working class lad from London. I'm not a person of pandemic Ill, harm or hatred. I have my own vernacular and that's one that sides and relates to those that question the two hallmarks of my culture, and that's those being of privilege and excessive wealth. It was a shared opinion with sir Winston Churchill who once said in a public address. "You drew your sword of freedom to cast away the shadows". The scoundrels I call friends are those same people. They question the greedy not the needy, the ones that are there and stand up for their own in any situation to do what's right, even when it's not easy. My actions and beliefs are open to criticism, but my integrity cannot be bought or bartered for.

I side with those that like me are of a cloth that is woven from lessons and experiences. My judgement is of primary colours and simple shades, I don't over exaggerate or complicate situations, nor do those I call friends. They set a benchmark and a standard on their responsibilities as a man and a person that installs a level of confidence and discipline on getting the job done. A close friend once said to me, "We do the wrong things for the right reasons, for the right people", and those that understand this, call them 'Lessons'.

A word from the wise-er

Liberalism is a mental disorder - **Michael Savage**

Success is going from failure to failure without losing enthusiasm - **Winston Churchill**

A man who loved his family and was ruthless to his enemies - **Richard the Lion Heart**

Man suffers only because he takes seriously what the gods made for fun - **Alan Watts**

A jug fills drop by drop - **Buddha**

There's never been a holy war fought in the name of Buddha - **Bobby Cummines**

Blood makes you related but loyalty makes you family - **Anon**

Question everything - **George Carlin**

A different branch, but from the same tree- **Paul Ferris**

If you're playing a poker game and you look around the table and you can't figure out who the sucker is, it's you - **Paul Newman**

French Fries come from Belgium- **Me!**

A little reminder to a well known 'crime' writer…….

A turkey is chatting with a bull.

"I would love to be able to get to the top of that tree," sighs the turkey, "but I just haven't got the energy."

"Well, why don't you nibble on some of my droppings?" replies the bull. "They're packed with nutrients"

The turkey pecks at a lump of dung and quickly finds that it actually gives him enough strength to reach the first branch of the tree.

The next day, after eating some more dung, he reaches the second branch.

Finally, after a week, there he is proudly perched at the top of the tree.

Unfortunately he is spotted by a farmer, who shoots him out of the tree.

Moral of the story: Bullshit might get you to the top, but it won't keep you there!

Introduction

SOME WORKING CLASS EAR 'OLE

It wasn't until I was five-years-old that I realised there were children and families that lived a different life from mine. That was when I was rudely dragged from my little council estate to attend the school in the village next to the town. Up until then my world-view ended at the roads in and out of our estate. Every family was not far off identical. Our houses were built the same and they contained (on the whole) a Mum, a Dad, some brothers and sisters, a dog and barely a motorcar between us. We played in the street until our mothers yelled us in for tea, a splash of children's TV and - when Dad got in from work – bed. We wore the same clothes: hand-me-down pullovers, shirts and shorts from our siblings with elbows darned to extend longevity.

Jason Allday

Once at school, although us boys and girls from the estate stuck together, we were in a minority and we were exposed to "class" for the first time. Not that I would have comprehended what it was at first but I knew it was something and that something crystallised as the years went by. That first year at school I witnessed my first "class" humiliation that has stayed with me. The school held a "Big Toy Day" where the kids were excused lessons for the day and allowed to carouse in the playground with their favourite big toy. It was a ritual. The boys from the private roads of nearby paraded shiny Claud Butler bikes, Johnny Seven guns, beautifully pressed Rawhide cowboy outfits and all sorts of other treasures to behold. We rolled in with trollies steered with string and constructed from discarded wood and pram wheels, bedraggled Action Men, Popeye glove puppets, toy monkeys and home-made, amateurishly painted totem poles. Even at that tender age we felt a strain of what I can now identify as shame.

I noted how, when asked where I came from and replied the Longmead Estate, teachers, adults and sometimes other children could not hide a change in facial expression. Sometimes I saw pity. Sometimes I saw distaste, sometimes I saw apprehension. I could not understand why. It was the best place to live. When I moved from infants' school to the junior one next door I started to mix with some of the non-estate boys. On visiting their houses, I saw that they were in tree-lined roads, were much bigger and grander and had tarmacked drives with cars parked imperiously on them. There were fridges and TVs that danced with colour and manicured Mums that asked us to remove our bumper boots before entering. There were strict curfews on wandering outside and we were encouraged to play Buckaroo or Subbuteo on the polished parquet floors. Life was a daily adventure of discovery then and I felt no discomfort at meeting and mixing with people who had different lives.

The first time I remember thinking through these differences was at age eleven. It was then we sat an exam called the eleven-plus that would decide what school we went to, who our adolescent friends would be and, to some extent, the rest of our lives. One hour-and-a-half long test of memory and an establishment cleaver drops and decides your fate forever. My father said to me in his later years that my failing my eleven-plus was a massive event in my life that he contended spurred me on to achieving certain things in adulthood. He said it made me rebellious and angry because my elder brother and sister had both passed.

My Dad spoke many words of wisdom but he was wrong here. I deliberately failed the exam. I looked at my best friends, especially dear Tony who lived around the corner and who I walked to and from school every day and who I had met standing on a drain as we were both punished for misbehaviour on our first day at infants' school, and knew they were not passing. I desperately wanted to continue to knock about with them and not go to the local grammar school where they wore little blue uniforms with caps. If you read The Beano we were Dennis the Menace and they were Walter. So, to questions like where was Jesus baptised, I wrote the Thames. My parents never believed this, but it was true.

From a class of thirty pupils about seven boys passed the exam. Not one of them was from our estate and all of them lived in the closes, cul-de-sacs and gardens of owner-occupier suburbia. I couldn't work that out. Why would where you lived dictate level of intelligence or memory or ambition?

About this time, I started to take an interest in my family history and for the first time I identified as working class. My mother's family came from a line of the rural poor. But they seemed to get by and there were examples of ancestors lifting themselves out of poverty. Her father, my granddad, became a skilled builder and ended up buying his own house. When my parents took the council house offered to them my mother agreed with my father on the condition that they saved up and got their own place rapido. My Dad could not see the rush – he was thrilled about having an indoor toilet and not sharing the house with three other families. They were still there forty years later.

Dad was from Battersea. Some may suggest that it was a family history littered with workhouses, suicide, unemployment, imprisonment and disease. One great uncle jumped off a London bridge to his death, weighted down with horseshoes, following despair at not being able to feed his family in the 1930's depression. Another died from malnutrition. My grandfather was a WW1 casualty. His sister-in-law and family members were killed in the 1940 bombing of Battersea and so on. It was a grinding existence. But the survivors I knew, like my grandmother who attained the age of 100, were happy, optimistic, strong and decent people. I don't know who it was, but someone suggested that my Dad, when he returned from WW2, flirted with communism but later self-educated and pursued a career in administration in the NHS. For a brief period in the 1970's I remember him being terrified of the rise of one Tony Benn. His childhood and distrust of stability never left him. I can recall him burying tinned food in the garden – preparing for the worst.

One family member, upon returning from the war charted a different course from my Dad. He grew up in arguably the poorest road in Battersea. His neighbours and best friends would become notorious in London's underworld – and they and my uncle saw things differently. When that same family member came home from the war he was bitter. Had they fought to maintain the status quo? A situation where 99% of the country toiled, starved and died while the other 1% owned all the land and resources having somehow constructed some pseudo wall of respect and deference around them. Like fuck he had. My uncle and his ilk had had enough and were not interested in trade unions and protests – they went on the other side and stayed there. He was a criminal for much of his life but a more honourable and decent person it will be hard to meet. Sounds bollocks, but true.

My prejudices deepened once I left school and entered the world of work. I was sixteen and after a period of idleness landed a job as a messenger boy at a leading daily newspaper. My Dad gave me some advice: "almost half of any workforce don't have or use their brain, the other half are bone idle. If you use your loaf you will get by. If you graft hard you will get by. If you do both, you'll clean up." He was right. Up to a point. I grafted and screwed my loaf. The days went quicker. And I steadily progressed through the newspaper to decent jobs in the library and business information departments. But then I would see graduates arrive and be placed automatically above me. I'd see others who had trouble spittling a stamp move past me in the organisation because they had attended a university. It was frustrating and incensed me. They'd smile patronisingly as they glided by.

This was the 1970's and industrial unrest was rife and in Fleet Street the trade unions were king. These same graduates were the most vocal and active in these daily battles. They read the Socialist Worker and traipsed off to Grunwick to add support to striking workers. They banged on about the plight of the working classes yet to a man (or woman) they came from privileged backgrounds. This never sat easily with me. They became union representatives and avoided all work they were being paid for as they wallowed in endless, pointless union business. Eventually, after some years and knowing there was only so far a working-class boy would ever go in this organisation, I left and set up on my own. I managed to have a very successful career in business and through that was able to indulge in my love of writing.

I was never sure about the label "working-class". For many periods throughout history the so-called working class have been deprived of the dignity of work, for one. I am now comfortable and live in a nice house with a shiny car on a tarmacked drive. Am I no longer working-class? I will argue I am. I see working class as a state of mind formed by heritage and attitude. I see myself in the context of my forebears. I see the class system diluted, but still there. We've had a prime minister from a poor, minimally educated background, ironically a Conservative, Mr Major. But only the one. But how many kids from council estates have reached the top in business? Why are the only roads out boxing and football? (Forget the latter) I believe that white, working-class kids now have it tougher than we did. Who is batting for them? Who dares? This section of society have been wrongly maligned through recent history. When we went out and got tattoos in the 1970's they were badges of belligerence, now all the Gavin's and Tristram's are sporting them – they are "cool" and arty. Our dogs are dangerous pets, their animals that are trained to hunt and kill foxes and deer are not. When we had a scrap at a football match we were hooligans. When they went bananas at a London demo they were protesting students.

But, I remember my estate and the others I frequented with or without rose-coloured spectacles. Community is an over-used, twisted word these days normally trotted out to denote a section of society who promote their "differenceness" and not integrating with the rest of us. But we had real community. When anyone on the estate died someone would knock on every door and collect money for a reef. When the hearse arrived at the house, we'd draw our curtains, or stand outside and bow our heads until the cortege left. We really did pop in and out of each other's houses borrowing sugar. We were comfortable with each other. The women folk standing outside chatting to one another, laughing and joking in the evenings as they walked to Bingo together. The men drank in the same pubs and or tended the same allotments proudly. These were real people some of who broke the law but most of who knew the difference between right and wrong. I would not change my upbringing for the world. It was fucking glorious.

So, what advice would I impart to young people on the wrong side of the Great Wall of Privilege today? I would say follow your dreams. As Alan Sillitoe (who I was fortunate enough to befriend) said in his seminal working-class novel Saturday Night, Sunday Morning – DON'T LET THE BASTARDS GRIND YOU DOWN. Take my old man's advice too. Work hard, think hard. Most of the others do not. Kick those barriers away. You're better than them.

Martin Knight

Book 1

Jason Allday

Enough is enough!

"Twenty pints a night, 22 red cards, 400 women and as many rows as the terrace hooligans of the 80's, and I have no regrets" - Roy

Red Card Roy captured the headlines, the eye of many a pretty girl and the brunt of his self induced, nitro-fuelled, fearless unorthodox approach to survival in the world of both semi-pro (non-league) and professional football. To sit and listen to Roy's jaw-dropping story of terrace fighting and pitch explosive antics, would inspire even the most conservative film makers, to seek reference to the banter and fight necessary, to show the raw edge of football. Roy is considered by many to be a cult hero - Britain's wildest ever footballer, who was sent off a record 22 times in a career of more than 650 games, 100 goals, thousands of beers and, allegedly, 400 women. From his first sending off, at an age of just 15, when he tried to strangle the referee in a school's cup final, Roy's life is best described as a rollercoaster ride of football, violence, sex and booze. Roy was far from someone that would capitulate to the requirements of the professional league, and its archaic protocols, as Roy would prove, his character far outweighed the industry standard of a 'yes boy'. Roy formed alliances with many professional footballers, and even with those he battled with on and off the pitch. Roy can even hold merit with the fact he formed an unlikely friendship with the late, great Bobby Moore. Of course, Roy's voice was not reserved for the greats in the game and certainly was not limited to his favourites in the world of football, as David Moyes, Martin O'Neill and Tony Pulis (who he punched to the floor after five minutes of an FA Cup tie) all felt the wraith of a young man from Solihull.

Lessons

Very few people can say they recognised that their lives were spiraling out of control and still enjoyed the ride. Roy's life is a textbook 'Use me as an example, not an excuse' story, but even looking back can find humour in the mass loss and betrayal he experienced from the industry. There was more than just early baths, brawls and beer. Roy's was a life that allowed a career driven talented athlete to really say 'I've been there, bought the t-shirt and torn the arse out of life'. All of this cost him the chance to play football at the very highest level. It was a common scenario that was frequent in his life as Roy once moved back and forth out of Colchester, Southend, Birmingham, Walsall, Exeter, Cambridge and, very briefly, Chelsea. Roy maintains a level of integrity and honesty, not excusing his past but identifying his losses, promoting the accomplishments and accepting the way his life was meant to be.

Jason Allday

Roy McDonough

"It's not that society is failing per se, it's that we have lions being led by donkeys"- Anon

The modern game isn't football. It certainly is not the game that was part of my life for over 30 years. It's become a non-contact sport. I mean, listen to the fans when they protest, and they have every right to with the money they're shelling out every week, just to see some tart prance about on a Saturday, pulling his socks over his knees, making sure he looks the part, and not dirtying his kit. I sometimes think the last thing on his mind is scoring a goal. That's been forgotten, that's (literally) being missed and that's the nuts and bolts of the game; putting yourself out there for your club, the shirt you're wearing and the fans who come and dedicate their money and time for you.

I was known as a person that would look for a bit trouble, but I see myself as a realist; a person that would put himself out to play a contact sport. People complain with the saturation of foreign-based players in the game, but sometimes I see some of those lads willing to get into the game and get themselves dirty. Image, greed, and the age-old pound note have destroyed a game I once gave my heart and soul for. My story is an easy one, the discipline was there, two hard working parents and family support, the right club and fans also were there when you wanted them to be, but it's heartbreaking to hear how a person without a scintilla of talent is favoured over a young player because he's not PC. I was never one to be bullied or would I roll over for the industry, not in a million years. Football is two teams of men, not mainstream industry, and mass-produced. plastic Charlie wannabes trying to be something they're not, and I can spot them a mile away. Look at football, it's men, human beings, that were once lads grown and raised as kids kicking a football about a field, typicaly after school or weekends, kicking the hell out of each other's shins and scoring a goal, and as such you're going to make mistakes during the game, accept it. That should be part of your agenda, caring for the game, becoming emotional and frustrated because you fought and made an effort to get the job done, and if and when your plan does fall through, just remember the goal will be in the same place when you get the ball back. I wouldn't at all be surprised in today's game of football, if some of the players went for a coffee enema and a therapy session after a game. Where's the balls and backbone gone!

Never apologise for taking a risk, or putting yourself in a non 'text book' situation. Look to be something more than just a 90-minute, pound note chasing twat. Fans deserve more than that, and the clubs are as much to blame for this. We invented the bloody game, and we're born with it in our blood, fucking fight hard, support your team mates and put the ball in the one place it's supposed to be, in the back of the net. Management are there to do an obvious job, and I'd be the first to get upset with them, simply because as I proved at one club, saving a team from relegation was more important than the manager's personal agenda. On the pitch, you're fighting a battle, not excessively worrying about image and sponsors, which should be second. Points keep a club up in the table, the players and fans deserve that, not a person that's never kicked a ball, who's only worried about his image and sponsored club car.

Footballers were heroes to me growing up, and Bobby Moore was one of them. Admittedly I'm hard to impress with those involved in football, but when I saw Bobby lift up that cup after the world cup win in 1966, I felt a great sense of pride and I've carried that memory since. He's probably one of the only players, I'd say, who didn't have to get in the mud to show he'd just slogged his guts out for a team. Thinking back when I watched the 1966 World Cup on the telly I saw the pitch and it'd been carved to pieces through 90 minutes of blood sweat and tears. It was real football, and there wasn't a single speck on the skipper's shirt. He never dived, gave in or went down easy. I met Bobby through a mutual while I was in a bar (you'd expect nothing less right!) And it was here I was to be signed up for Southend under the care of Bobby Moore. A dream come true, as he was god-like to me from my childhood. For the first time in a very long while, I didn't turn up on Bobby's watch looking or feeling like the back end of a bad weekend. Bobby was a man that simply lived up to the hype, a truly talented player that was more brain and less muscle in the game. No words could ever justify the skill and passion that man brought, day in day out.

It was the F.A cup 3rd round, and as fate would have it, someone that I owed a score with was playing on the other team. I'd assured Bobby before the game I was going to behave; as I'd made it publicly known I was going to settle the score with the other player. My intentions were there, I respected Bobby more than any other player, but my anger and premeditated agenda took over, like the colour red to a bull. My actions cost the other player being injured, me being carded and fined and the loss of the game, I've often thought of that red card and send off more than any other day, I'm not one for regrets but that's probably one of only two red cards I can mention. Another ex West Ham player that I rated was Harry Cripps. The irony is that he got his name as a talented; no bullshit player at West Ham's rivals Millwall. As for managers, that's easy Bobby Moore, no question! He was a footballer and then some, also Bobby Charlton; both were a credit to their positions. And it's a very difficult position to hold being once a player then the manager, as sacrifices are made when in that position and you can't be 'a nice guy'.

Thoughts on me and the greatest game ever played? I'd have to say the best and worst person I played against on and off the pitch was myself, I truly found my soul in football, and I was never intimidated by those without a scintilla of talent, and I've played a lot of people but the irony was my one freedom in life in-prisoned me - football. I'll never forget a lesson from my early days, and one of a few times when I've thought how cruel and unforgiving the game could be. I was signed on at Chelsea, and that was one of London's biggest clubs and from this you'd think it'd be the dog's bollocks, but here I was left to suffer in silence. There is no other way I see or remember that experience, in fact I'd say it was what was supposed to be my Camelot, and it was at Chelsea that I nearly quit the game. It had poor management, a weak structure set up, and this was totally disheartening to a young footballer. It was supposed to be my step up from Walsall and almost become my step out from the game.

There are always comments on hindsight, the 'what ifs' and 'that old chestnut', but I can't and won't let that effect me. Alcohol combined with football brought out the best and worst in me. You can't buy experience, and I've learned and accepted that I was abusing myself, and was basically filling a vacuum because of how I was treated by the industry. I needed the buzz, and whether you interpret it as a positive or a negative effect, I found that escape in woman and drink. One thing I hold true is I never abused the women, and yes there was a few along the way. How I treated myself was a different story, but as much as I was a womaniser I always tried to treat the woman by my side with the respect she deserved.

The money involved in today's game is just mind blowing and injuries while being paid gets me. I'm not here to blow my own trumpet, but in one season at Southend FC, and remember it was the same year we got promoted, I played 41 games, I only missed 5 down to suspensions, I averaged 75 to 85 pints of Stella a week and no injuries, what does that tell you? Dedication to the game has changed which is again down to money. It has seriously destroyed the sport, and I think it's fair to say it created not only a different type of player, but also a different perception and lack of respect for the sport.

My actions were my own, but I promise you it's a shared opinion with any footballer that's worth his boots, on the modern game and the industry leaders who call themselves the ones in charge. I stood up and voiced what was right and wrong. How can anyone be faulted over honesty; as its honesty that's the best offense for bullshit! What I saw wrong with a team, the management or the structure, I expressed in my own way. As for a closing thought for my fans, play the game you know how, be yourself, respect there's more than just you on the pitch and for fuck sake, just put the bloody ball in the back of the net.

My father, the hero

Eric Mason was a once known and still a respected man within the underworld. A person of such principal, that to reinforce his belief of the unjust brutality within the prison system, he would himself cause a stir so as to be counted along side a friend that had under come the once known and documented viciousness from prison officers. A person of such integrity, he would take part of the punishment, so a lesser man in standing wouldn't feel he was alone in a fight or isolated in a world that prison can easily promote.

It's a fact that many have a shared respect and admiration for a once known player amongst the leaders of the old school, so what knowledge could a friendship give anyone in terms of a positive influence? It's easy, a no brainer, in fact it's as easy as counting the fingers on your hand! A father's love and dedication in raising his children can be seen and a testament to Eric Mason with his son Michael. That life long commitment and education Michael received from his father has enabled him to be a compliment to his father's teachings.

In a person's life, managing the frustrations and tempestuous challenges of life can be one of peril. These same challenges have faced Michael undeservingly more than once and learning to deal with the consistent barrage of hate, fate and unfairness life can indiscriminately throw at a person is something, that is in some cases hard to justify. These challenges aren't unique to Michael's life, but knowing how to 'roll with the punches', is something that is a talent that as a result of his father's discipline has allowed Michael to come out on top each and every time. Michael shares this with not only myself but proudly with his own family. He carries a hardened childhood that was filled with the principals on what was and will always be respected by the old guard. Integrity, respect and dedication are part of Michael's daily discipline. These qualities are learned, certainly not given lightly or bought. No fool can carry this level of confidence and experience, only someone that listened and followed the rules. Friends and family's personal needs and best interests take president over Michael's needs and wants. I was once told a dedicated father makes a man. With a great sense of pride, I call Michael a friend and a clear example of a chip off the old block, a living testament to the late great Eric Mason, who once moved in all the right circles, top drawer, quality people. With modern day society and the very system that struggles to maintain a level of discipline with youths of today, it's a strong-shared belief that there's lessons to be learned and a standard that should be modeled on with the old school.

Michael Mason

"In crime, I find a semblance of reality"- Anon

"I was born in Manchester in 1985, and named Michael Patrick Mason. My dad, Eric Mason, was a well-known and respected person in the criminal world. Dad had settled and met my mum while she was working at a club he frequented. She said my dad always had an aura around him and people would always warp towards him, she never asked what he did nor did she care, she just loved him for him. Not because he was a gangster, because in hindsight she has hated how much trouble I have gotten myself into since being a teenager and continuing through my 20's. Had I not been Eric Mason's son, and my dad any other man, I've often wondered how and where I'd learned what was needed to get me through the hurdles I've had to face. One thing I know is I'm proud of my dad and I hope he's looking down on me with a shared pride. Early memories as a child for me were in some respects different than most children. For me being the son of a known villain allowed me to see some real heavy-duty people. Real men who played by a shared set of principles and rules and knew how to treat a woman. What was fun for me as a child was these faces from Manchester, Blackpool and London would give me countless amounts of money. When ever we would go somewhere we paid for nothing and I thought this was normal. The irony was my dad actually shielded us from his criminal life, but I always could tell everyone loved, respected or in some cases feared my dad.

Jason Allday

My dad named me after a legend from Blackpool, who he met in Dartmoor prison in the 1950's when at the time they were the two youngest prisoners in that horror house. His name was Michael 'Mixie' Walsh. Now there's a man that was a real inspiration to me. Mixie was a testament to what a gentleman and a fighter was all about. It's common- place today to hear and sometimes see a fighter losing a fight and then pulling a knife. Mixie's style was nothing short of a gentleman and a fighter, pure quality! He'd often be offered-out by another fighter, and Mixie would oblige. The fight would be taken to another location and some time after they'd both return and have a drink with each other. That right there demands respect. Both mum and dad said he was one of the kindest most honorable people you could have wished to of known, my mum still lights up when you speak of Mixie. As a fighting man, he was one of the best street fighters that you would encounter. He was also a keep fit fanatic and was Mr. Blackpool. He was very well known amongst people in the south as a hard but equally as fair man. A good few like-minded and respected men that moved in the criminal world have mentioned Mixie. I have some good memories of Mixie and I'm honored to carry his name. R.I.P a child hood hero of mine Michael 'Mixie' Walsh.

So, we had a back and fourth routine from our home in Manchester and our second home in Blackpool, but it was as though we had a third home in Spain. We would go all the time I loved it out there. Again, at the time and as a child I never understood how my dad knew everyone and they knew my dad. It was no coincidence they all talked with London accents and greeted each other the same way. I was soon to discover in my older years that they were criminals who had either made their fortune and gone to retire in the sun or they were on the run for serious crimes. Looking back now and knowing the company I was in as a child, it's strange for me because these men were the most respectful men you would meet. The woman and children were looked after well, yet normal society would class them as monsters. I suppose it's just the world you live in and I only ever saw great men who taught me to play pool and let me win. It was the best of times, and we had fantastic memories all over Spain; Costa Del Sol, Mijas, Marbella, Mijorca, Fuengirola to name but a few. I would come back from these places with wads of money, as for me it was just the norm'.

Lessons

My dad was a fighting man and being he was also a fanatical boxing fan he had gloves on me from the time I was able to walk. I remember he would get on his knees use is hands as jab pads, he would love doing that with me and did it with me all threw my child hood, the discipline and necessary requirements required in boxing is something I saw with dad. One of the reasons I've never shied away from a fight is because my dad always told me always use your fists and never back down to a bully, which I'm thankful for. The training and discipline dad instilled in me as a child paid off. I can throw a mean left and right and that has helped me out a few times. I think the fighting stems from his own childhood as a result of being placed in an approved school. This was for young delinquents and dad was about 13 years old. Here he suffered years of abuse both physical and sexual at the hands of the priests that ran the school. It sickens me to think what they did to my dad in that place. I remember on one occasion he told me, had it not been for the years he spent in the sadistic perverse regime, his life may have taken a different turn, but he left St. Vincent's with a lot of hate towards the system and authority, not only because of what happened to him, but what he witnessed others go threw as the priests encouraged older boys to molest the younger ones. So, he always said he felt that he had to stand up for the weaker guy and never let a bully or authority win over him. It's these principles that have stuck with me and I shall pass onto my son Harry, who is at the age now where soon the gloves will be out and the circle will continue.

When I was roughly 5 years old my dad went away. I asked my mum where he had gone? She told me he was at work and wouldn't be back for a while. The safety and security that was once there was now gone. That time alone is one of I'd never experienced, and if honest would never allow my own children to experience. I later found out when I was older that he was in prison for a fraud charge. This was the first time he'd tried with all his heart and soul to lead a straight life. The business fell apart around him. In the straight every day working world there can be as many criminals as my dad had worked with in his other life. The money he was owed he never got and in desperation got caught up in a fraud scam. Life sometimes isn't fair but you learn to deal with it. I remember he was gone for what seemed like forever. Then one day he appeared on the street, my dad was home and we was off doing the rounds again. I always came alive when I was with him, a real child hood hero. It's what every son deserves; the security, closeness and relationship you'd dream of but some of us are not dealt a fare hand in the game of life.

I like to think while my dad was in prison he had time to reflect and maybe began to weigh up the amount of time he had spent inside. He always cared for us, and I feel when he was with us and maybe looking at me and seeing how Manchester's gun culture was changing, he didn't want it for his family. So, we moved to Yorkshire and a town called Harrogate, a far cry from any city and since then has been a home for me with my own children. It was the best thing ever. I have no doubt that growing up in Manchester with just the reputation I have accumulated in a town like Harrogate, I would be either of been doing a huge jail sentence or I'd be dead. As my life stands now, I have too much to live for. Two beautiful children Mia and Harry aged 3 and 2 only, 11 months apart and they are my life. As we got settled into Harrogate my dad started receiving phone calls from two friends, one called Ronnie and another called Reggie. He would put me on the phone, and after he'd said, "say hello to my boy, Reg' " I would get a reply "hello, I hope you're keeping your dad out of trouble!" I would just say what any kid would say, "of course, he's my dad" and in my mind my hero, and then the same when Ronnie rang. My mum still says to this day when Ronnie Kray would ring that he would say "Oh hello, lovely to speak with you. May I ask, is Eric there please?" Very well mannered, but she would add after "you could tell well, what he was just over the phone". Back then my dad would say "don't be daft it's only Ron". Having grown up with the twins and seeing them in their hey-day and the many business dealings with them, dad always told me he was a lot closer to Reggie purely for that fact that some times he didn't agree with Ronnie's erratic behavior and he said he felt that Reggie and Charlie in some instances paid the price for being Ronnie's brother. My dad did say Ronnie was one of the kindest men you would meet. If a woman couldn't pay for her shopping he would give her one hundred pounds like it was nothing. Money had no value to him. Dad said the twins were both very unique in their ways and he saw them try and better each other many times, but would die for each other in a fight against an outsider. It was at the time he was receiving these phone calls that he began writing a book himself. My sister had not long been born and I would sit on his knee while he wrote on a note pad. I asked him what he was writing and he replied, "I'm writing about my life, son". I asked, "why dad?" I would come to understand when I was older what and why. Life's lessons and those that prompt you to question your integrity is something that needs to be passed on. It was also at this time I started noticing scars on my dad's body, not just tiny scars but horrific scars. One day when we were in the garden, he took his shirt off and I noticed huge scars on his back. I asked what they were. He explained that were given to him by cowards who couldn't fight him. I was later to find out they were scars from the cat-o-nine tails. A punishment he received in prison for attacking 4 officers. He was the last man in England to receive that punishment. He had also been birched many times as a child at St Vincent's. When I think about my own experiences in prison, it makes me realise no wonder these men were so tough, because going threw that experience and surviving and not crumbling you would have to one hard bastard not to have been broken. Prison then and now is so different. It was also around this time I started to realise my dad wasn't like other dads. I noticed other scars on his hands and wrists. When I asked what they were he said that he had had a fight with people who had to use weapons to beat him. I was later to find out he was kidnapped as part of a gang-war and nearly killed by 8 men with knifes and axes. My dad never grassed, never looked for an easy out, never blamed anyone for the decisions he'd made; lessons.

Things were going good, my dad was back and fourth, he was keeping busy and on occasion he would come back with a boot full of toys. We set up a punch bag in our garage and we would do bag drills on it then he would go running for miles, not forgetting this was a man in his 60's. We would still go to Blackpool and Manchester to see Mixie and a few other faces. There was a time in Blackpool when I first saw my dad and Mixie chin two guys in a pub. My mum said Mixie would have people come from all over the country wanting to fight him and he would always accept. She said he would be back in the pub in a minute and the guy would be buying him a drink shaking his hand after just being knocked spark out. One particular time my sister and I happened to be there when two fellas came in and asked, "Are you Mixie Walsh?", he replied, "Yes!" " We want to fight you they said". Now Mixie was the type of man that you couldn't swear in front of a woman but something must have really irritated him. Memory serves me well on this occasion as to my surprise his words were "fuck off,

I'm with company!" Anyone that knew Mixie would've or should've known he was clearly bothered. These clowns obviously didn't and paid for their mistake. They continued to push their personal agenda and the men simply wouldn't listen. Then like a jack in the box both my dad and Mixie jumped up hit them both on their chins knocking them both clean out. It was almost comical, like one of the old saloon fights in the western films. Mixie picked one up and threw him outside and my dad picked up the other one and stamped him into place where there was a space between the fruit machine and the bar now making him part of the fixture. He then calmly returned to his seat and carried on with his G and T. I remember looking at my dad and just thinking he is the hardest man around, I idolised him. There's a time and a place for most things, what those two clowns wanted, was being demanded for in the wrong place at the wrong time, another lesson.

I started noticing other things' as I got older. We would be in a pub and someone would come in to speak with my dad and as a result the men in the bar would change the conversation from the 'family type' and then once business was discussed and settled they'd come back to the original conversation. Subtle changes in mannerisms and context but something I'd always remember. I remember once walking into the bedroom at our house and my dad and his friend were in there and the amount of money on the bed covered it. I was told to shut the door and go play outside.

Christmas times we got everything, birthdays those too were some amazing times but then something awful happened. My dad had just bought his book out the 'The inside story' I was 11 or so and my mum who had two sons from a previous marriage, the eldest, my half brother David, who I worshipped was sadly suffering from some mental health problems and didn't get the help he needed and sadly committed suicide leaving behind two children of his own. It devastated me and still to this day I think of him. I will always miss him. We had Dave's funeral and wake at a 5-star hotel given to us for free as a mark of respect to my mum and dad by one of their friends. It was a sad day, everyone mourning and I remember my mum saying her and my dad was going for a quiet drink together just down the road at another friend's pub. My memory and mind lead me to believe someone very close to me was drained and distraught. What Happened next was something that has stuck in my head forever. There was an incident at the pub, that resulted in someone getting abuse from a certain person (thankfully not related). I won't mention them by name but will go as far to say they are just a bunch of scumbag alcoholics. Next thing I know insults were thrown and before I knew the entire room erupted into a full-on brawl with chairs, tables, glasses and fists getting thrown everywhere. My seven-year-old sister was trapped in the middle of it all but thankfully a female friend dived on her to shield her while someone was stamping on her head. It was inevitable that it would escalate and before long it spilled into the street. A lot of people ended up in hospital with serious injuries. Then my mum and dad appeared. My dad went absolutely berserk. That was my brothers send off and I'll say certain people that day were an utter disgrace. Know that if I came across anyone of these that caused that much hurt and disrespect today I would happily break their jaws.

So, a month down the line and we started to take trips to Spain. I think my dad was just trying to take my mums mind of things but it wasn't working. About a month later my dad left us and moved back to Manchester, I was gutted. I would go see him on weekends but the woman he lived with I couldn't stand. As time went on months turned into years and all I wanted was to see my dad more then ever, then another blow hit me. He was locked up for a major drug conspiracy charge where an undercover copper had been in with this crew for four years. They were fucked! My dad was sent to prison for 6 years after a year on remand.

Now by this point I had already started going of the rails myself. I had discovered drugs; cannabis, ecstasy and cocaine. I also discovered I had a lot of miss placed anger and I started getting into a lot of bother. It wasn't long before a friend and myself were getting into low-level crime and from there it escalated, there was nothing we wouldn't do together. Now it wasn't a question of if, just when. I was 16 years old when I got my first taste of prison. I was in a bar in my town and they knew I was under age but the owner didn't dare not let me in. I came out of the bar and two older men were attacking a friend of mine. I knocked them out, turned only to see out another guy strike the girl I was seeing at the time, resulting in a serious head injury. I simply lost it and I started knocking 7 bells out of him. In the process I looked round and a guy was running directly at me. I thought it was one of their friends, so I went straight for him, resulting in him getting knocked out. From here it got worse, as it just so happened he was a plain cloths copper (it was worth it). I got my girlfriend by the hand and we got away but the entire incident was on CCTV. I was arrested for a violent disorder after being on the run for a month, though luckily enough they couldn't do me for the assault on the police officer because he wasn't in uniform and from what I understand he failed to identify himself as a policeman. I was far from being in the clear, as whilst awaiting trial for this, the drug abuse got worse. A friend of mine was arrested for something and being the person I am, I took it upon myself to help a friend in need. I went to the guy's house, kicked his door off and threatened him with serious repercussions if he took it further. Un be known to me there was someone sat in the corner of the room. First chance they had, they made a complaint to the police. I was now on witness intimidation and a violent disorder charge. I new I was fucked but I didn't care, it was, what it was. At this time some of the older people in my town started asking if I was related to Eric Mason. When I said yes, he's my dad their jaws would hit the floor in addition, how they acted towards me changed. I hated it, as I wanted my own name and my own earned respect. I now felt I had something to prove when deep down I really just wanted my old man back on the streets and to be part of his life. I would get the odd phone call and letter but it was never enough. When I got sentenced at crown court, I got the violent disorder luckily dropped to an affray but was advised to go guilty on the witness intimidation. I plead guilty to both and was told to expect nothing less than three years, I got a year, I was happy. I spent my 18th birthday in a young offenders institution while my dad spent his 74th birthday 2 days later in HMP Garth, what were the odds of that eh? I entered prison and kept my nut down and invested my time into weight lifting. So, in some respects I came out of prison with more than I went in with. Thinking back the weights and my self-discipline has saved me from my demons. The years went on and I've found myself in situations resulting in more court cases. Typically, it's related to GBH or ABH charges. I've gotten out of them, as I was clearly innocent. Though other arrests and charges would surface including supplying substances and money laundering. As it happened there was no evidence but all this time I wasn't thinking of the effects it was having on my mum. She had lost one son already and on top of all of this my dad finally got released but this prison term had aged him terribly. Dad and I went on the piss and had an amazing night it was the first time I met my dad's eldest son, my half brother Jeff. We clicked instantly and we had some session. It wasn't long after this the police caught up with me for a violent crime and I went on the run to Blackpool. My dad's health was deteriorating rapidly and I could see he had Alzheimer's, it killed me to see him like that but soon I had no money and the police were harassing people's houses for me. It was time to hand myself in, I was put on remand but after a month the witness changed their mind. I was released and started seeing an old flame. She fell pregnant and when my daughter was born she was born with an extremely rare life-threatening illness. Two weeks later my dad died, I had two choices, stand up and be a fucking man or wallow and say why me? Well, I'm a Mason! So, what do you think I chose? I'm proud to say I've fought this daily battle every waking moment with my little girl ever since, she's due to have her kidney transplant very soon. I also have a son who in my eyes is a blessing, because there was a chance he could have had the same illness but he's a strong boisterous amazing character. He was conceived a week after my dad died. Now I'm not superstitious but I think that everything in that 6 weeks have given me the strength to become what I am today. I know my dads fighting spirit lives on in my daughter.

If I was ever to be asked my opinion on today's failing society it would be with the drug culture. Not so much your weed smokers (smoking itself is something I despise) but more your hard drugs; class A's. When I see these degenerates begging on the streets it's not because of bad luck in life, it's a moral decision they've made and want your everyday working class to compensate for their filthy habits. This is where the government should step in. You're on a benefit than if you're not disabled, a wounded veteran or a mum with children to look after and care for than they should have to work for their benefits. Where's the incentive for a smack head to get them selves in order other than of course lining up for people's tax money? If I were asked on how to contribute, I'd start within the schools. Boxing is a sport I've always admired. A sport followed by kings and princes not ponces and low lives. Test your courage and dedication by enrolling in a boxing club. It was part of a lot of respected villains young lives. That was of course before your liberal brigade stepped in. Look how that's turned out! A sport in a child's life is as healthy and as necessary as geography and maths.

Jason Allday

One thing a lot of villains despised was a low-life junkie. Just look at the villains of past and the moral standard that they set and lived by, government and mainstream have their opinion on them and so do I. Class, pure fucking class! Suited and booted, integrity and respect, a lot can be said about the top chaps of yesteryear and I can assure you there's a lot more negative I can say about today's society. Pros and cons, you weigh it up! How does it make you feel when you're walking down your local high street with your children and to see that waste of a human soul sitting and begging? It sends a message to children, their actions say, 'if all else fails, and life gives you a hurdle, don't worry you have an option by begging for a fix'. I used to take great pleasure taxing drug dealers, as most knew me and those that were blatant about their disgusting trade paid me. No options, no ifs, no butts! Low lives all of them. Destroying lives is all it does. Too many options and excuses in my humble opinion for young minds to fail as when it's time to leave school than the options should be continued education or national service. Discipline needs to be instilled within young minds. The old school, like my dad, lived by a universal code, that when understood and accepted simply meant manners and respect was a standard in every person's everyday practice. There are more options and opportunities now than ever with the world being a smaller place. This was a conversation I had just recently with a trusted pal from London. It's common place that we all hear how the old school has gone. That the old guard and the values they once invested in society is a thing of the past and that how people were there for those in need. Well one thing we both agreed on is that these same principles and morals are still there and in fact never went anywhere, instead, now the only difference is they are more protected and valued, as too many people took advantage of peoples generosity but know that if and when the help is needed for the right person and the right reason a phone call is all that is needed to show there is not loss but a chance.

One man I must thank is Jason Allday, who I'm proud to call a friend and true man with morals. We represent different parts of the country, some shared friends within certain circles but proud that we both were given a standard set of principles clearly showing that the integrity of the people we learned from, lives on."

Lessons

One of the strongest bodies a man could hold, lost his battle to the demons within - the darkness claimed another soul. On the 16th of April 2016, word was given that Michael Mason was taken from us all. Over the few years I'd gotten to know him, he'd always spoken of his loyalty and love for his children and a shared value of the rights and wrongs he'd learned from his late father, Eric Mason. It was an honor to have had Michael as a friend. Sleep well, mukka. - Jase

RIP Michael P. Mason
July 1985-April 2016

Jason Allday

It's in the blood

Martin King was as much a fixture at the Shed as the turnstiles leading into the ground. For over four decades, Martin invested not only time and passion but literary blood sweat and tears, for a team he calls his family. Like most of those that dedicated the weekly visit, which is more than your modern-day arm chair brigade, Martin knows more on what is someone's right to call themselves a true fan of Chelsea. Martin can also tell you something, on what I'd happily question any modern-day fan on and that's difference between the value, cost and responsibility as a supporter of your chosen club. All the years visiting Chelsea at the bridge and the away games all meant something. This of course meant his father, his family and those that loved the game. Those that are universally known as your own.

There's a lot to be said about the relationship between a lad and football. In my mind, it's a sense of belonging. In my experience there was three important factors as a fan. Of course, football. Fashion and music followed closely; though there's always been a debate in what order of the last two come in! There's pride and passion to be spoken of, especially when it involves an iconic London club. Even more so when your dad is interwoven within that history; as without family, what do you have?

My omission and honesty is my dad and both grandfathers were arsenal and Chelsea fans! Thankfully I was saved; Mums family of course east London; West Ham. One thing I agreed on with my grandfathers at an early age, was fishing would be the only social sporting tie and not the supporting of their teams.

If there's something that can be spoken on with both shared pride and a sense of dedication with Martin, and that's the memories that hold from his time spent as a son and a fan to the Bridge. Football holds more to some and it's easily seen and heard with Martin. The rows, the clothes and the history are all part of the parcel. Martin speaks well of those that hold merit and value in his life. Both on and off the terraces there's stories to be told. Thankfully the real losses and results of his experiences have not been given in a biased way. As I've always said, those that claim to have never come unstuck, were either not there or living in a delusional world.

A true sense of measure is warranted only by the memories you have as a fan. Martin scored high here. Few sports promote such an outlet for a fan. It can be easily seen when your team is down, the fans put out the call to the players and when the result that is needed comes in, no sport other than football allows such a euphoric emotion to be displayed. All of this interwoven within the fabric of a person's life gives something to be marveled at. For it is then you can say you championed the art of being both a fan and a supporter.

Jason Allday

Martin King

"Modus operandi; we are who we are" – Anon

The men were playing cards in my Nan's kitchen, three card brag & rummy was the game of their choice, while us kids sat and watched the 1965 Cup Final at Wembley between Liverpool and Leeds Utd. I remember Ron Yeats the Liverpool centre half towered above Leeds captain Bobby Collins before the start of the game which Liverpool won by 2 goals to 1. Names like Roger Hunt and Ian St. John and Ian Gallaghan and a young Tommy Smith were then the golden boys of English football and I remember this was the first cup final to feature Albert Johanneson a black player.

I was 9 years old and my mind was like a sponge when it came to football. A few years earlier my Dad who was a mad sports fan took me to watch the double winning Spurs team, beat Nottingham Forest 4 – 1. The following week he took me to watch his team Fulham at Craven Cottage and the week after that we were off to watch Chelsea play Manchester United in front of 67,000 fans. I loved it. Back home on that Saturday night we watched Match of the Day on our old black and white telly, eating our fish and chip supper. The old man turned to me and asked me which team I was going to support, as quick as a flash I answered Chelsea, so the next day he knocked me up a blue and white wooden rattle with Chelsea painted down one side. I was over the moon and he was out in the back garden waving it above my head making an awful racket and annoying the neighbours.

Going to watch Chelsea with my Dad was now a regular thing and we even went to a few away games. Coming out of the ground after a London derby against Arsenal I noticed a few kids hanging around on the steps opposite Fulham Broadway. They seemed to be a bit different from other supporters, over the course of that season I always saw them hanging around. I asked my Dad who they were, "they're young Herbert's looking for bother", that was it I wanted to be a "Herbert".

It wasn't long before I was going to football with older lads from school. This was around the time of the start of the late 60's Skinhead fashion. I was spending my hard-earned paper round money on Harrington Jackets, Crombie's, Ben Sherman, Brutus and Jaytex shirts, Dr Martin boots and Levi-sta-press trousers. Now I looked the part and could stand in The Shed at Chelsea and not look out of place. Us London boys looked the dog's bollocks at games not like them scruffy fucking Northerners that came to our place for matches. They didn't have a clue how to dress with their long hair, baggy scruffy dirty jeans, and donkey jackets, they reminded me of a load of greasers, and I did hear that the Scousers lead the way in terrace fashion? Don't make me laugh they didn't have a clue on how to dress, they looked like a right bunch of tramps when they came to the Bridge for a game. Just the thought of them claiming to have stated the casual movement at football is laughable.

My school friends started mixing with some older and wiser lads from around the Tooting area that claimed to be close friends of Greenaway and Eccles the two recognised leaders of The Chelsea Shed that was good enough for me. You see it was all about trust at football, it didn't matter how brave or game you were, at the end of the day it was about having good reliable people around you, who wouldn't let you down at the first sign of trouble. Where I came from we had a lot of Travelling or Gypsy boys who had started to come to football with us Mitcham lads, and fighting was a way of life for them, it was like their national sport and most of them wouldn't know a football from a golf ball or even a billiard ball, they were only there for the rucks and were as game as fuck.

Jason Allday

Over the years I've met some great fellas going to football and have had a fair old few scrapes but we were never bullies. We knew who wanted a fight and the other mob likewise. It's like two boxers in a ring they know who they're there to fight and it ain't the referee. Hitting women, children or the anoraks in football shirts are not a legitimate target. Sadly, for some people they are. I've heard of Tottenham fans attacking women and blokes with their kids in Chelsea shirts. How brave is that? Another bunch of cowards are Swansea. Myself and a visually impaired pal were drinking with our mate and his nephew with a few older Swansea boys when a group of about 40 Swansea young lot came in and started giving it the large one. Their supposedly main man challenged me to a fight but was soon back peddling when I told him "let's get it on". He was a big mouthed bully with no arsehole. Then one of them glassed me from behind and another one of theirs tried hitting blind pal over the head with a bottle. Before you knew it, they were off back to Paddington and on the train back to Wales, not even bothering to go to the game. Low-life scum, that's all they are.

Recently they beat up a 15-year-old boy with autism and put him in hospital after a Swansea V Chelsea game. He and his older brother were walking back to the railway station after the game, minding their own business when they were attacked by a mob of Swansea fans. How very brave?

This new breed of casual; at games need to learn the rules of combat and not every opposing fan is a legitimate target. The old bill are quick to jump on so called racist chanting and foul language when women, young kids and normal Joe public are having the granny beat out of them by nothing more than knob-headed scumbags. There used to be a code at football but sadly this new breed have abandoned that and are glorifying their sad behaviour whilst sitting on their keyboards boasting to their mates and the world on just how hard they are, all from the safety of their bedrooms. Little Johnny or little Taffey in their Stone Island jumpers or CP Goggle coats are today's heroes of the terraces. How sad is that? – Wankers!

Simply Look back on the level of understanding we employed when it came to wanting to have a go. If that still existed today, if half the so-called hoolifans had any courage at all, they'd see there is a difference. It even went as far as your rivalries weren't carried into everyday life. With a London derby and half the clubs within a stones throw of each other, you'd never get anything accomplished if it carried over from and away from the terraces. The unwritten rules remained in place Id say up until the mid eighties. There's opinions on why, but in my opinion the need to get in and get the job done was intensified with CCTV and the unnecessary lengthy prison surrounding a row between like minded fans.

Football brought a lot of people together. And so did the music scene. The '80's bought the rave scene and it's believed this was the first progressive type of music that allowed fans to get along. What's unfairly missed is the convergence of blacks and whites much earlier than this. The wave of Jamaican immigrants brought many first-generation black English youths to share common interests with a lot of people I went to football with. It's a fact that in the '60's and '70's, both black and white kids shared the same streets to play on, danced in the same clubs, shared a passion for the same music and also the fashion, that I still believe was influenced to a degree by 1st generation black English youths. They even carried it with a credible degree of style. There was no animosity as even back then with my skin head and dr. Martin boots a simple stroll through Brixton market never caused a stir or malice from either cultural back ground towards each other. The late 1970's far right-wing groups fucked all that up, and as main stream media can be counted on, fueled a lot of total bollocks and media lies, but that's nothing new. In fact, I can remember a visit to Upton Park where there was more discrimination between the two clubs than colour. If you were Chelsea, you were fucked and the same mentality was extended from Chelsea toward west ham, as really any club back then.

Here's one that's crystal and can't be better described in terms of those that are up for it and have the same agenda. On a visit to Cardiff, we were given the opportunity to have it out with their main firm. The Taffs are as game as they come and have healthy numbers. Plenty of verbal was exchanged during the match from both sides. So, there was no confusion on who wanted to have a go. Upon exiting the ground, we headed towards a park that had a decent sized amount of Cardiff supporters waiting for us. They knew we was coming and we had the same mind set and agenda. There was no confusion in what was about to happen. Even the Cardiff old bill were decent and fair, if you got your collar felt it was fair game across the board; they'd nick Cardiff as evenly as Chelsea hooligans. With the police escort to and from the game, not once was there any bullying or looking for an easy target. You'd be a complete mug, in both mine and anyone's eyes that respects himself and those in it for a row. Know the difference, be a fan, be a hooligan, be what you will but again, know there's a difference in who you are and be a man not a bully.

    Martin King
    Base camp Mount Everest 2015.

Dirty Babylon?

"If we desire respect for the law, we must first make the law respectable"- Louis D. Brandies

It's inevitable during your lifetime, you will encounter a person that's been entrusted to uphold the laws of our country, and paid to protect your best interests. Whether it be a simple traffic violation, in need of assistance, or to protect and serve, the police are a necessary part of the very structure we live by every day. It's important that I point out that this isn't an O.B bashing venture, and everything written and contributed is factual and for the reader to simply decide right or wrong.

There hasn't been a country in the world that doesn't have reports of police conflict, including brutality and in some occasion's actual deaths. In the UK from 1990 through 2012, there were almost 1,000 deaths of people while in police custody; this doesn't include shootings, road traffic incidents and pursuits, so where does the accountability fall? With each and every detainee, there is a very specific process on anyone being held in custody. As equally important as the detainee, the arresting police officer(s) and those involved, is the recording of their information. Again, due process, independent investigation units, a paper trail and CCTV should thwart any misdoings, but even with all of the fail-safes in place, there's still loss of life. So, the question remains, why?

On April 1st 2009, Ian Tomlinson was killed during a baton attack by PC Harwood. As a result, Mr. Tomlinson died on the city street. An investigation led to a not guilty verdict on the manslaughter charge. Mr. Tomlinson, was pushed and then struck from behind by the PC as he walked away from a police line in the City of London during the G20 protests, he later collapsed and died. The last time a police officer was successfully prosecuted for the death of somebody in custody was in 1969, when two Police officers responsible for the death of David Oluwale, the first black man to die in police custody in the UK, were successfully prosecuted. This should have been a mile stone event, but to date, no police have been prosecuted, or convicted of the death of someone whilst in police custody.

An officer's oath

All police officers wishing to be public servants are required to stand in front of an appointed public official and be sworn in prior to any public service. A police constable swears this oath in a ceremony before a Justice of the Peace (Magistrate) who then grants them a Warrant card. The warrant card awards the constable his/her authority - on condition they uphold their sworn oath. Nowhere does it state or does this privilege allow a police officer to abuse this trust in an appointed public post, that is under as much scrutiny as public dependency, there should never be on the officer's part any confusion between responsibility and authority, a trained official should be able to discriminate the difference between the two.

Section 83 of the Police Reform Act 2002 requires all UK Police officers to swear the following oath of office:

"I, ... of .. .. do solemnly and sincerely declare and affirm that I will well and truly serve the Queen in the office of constable, with fairness, integrity, diligence and impartiality, upholding fundamental human rights and according equal respect to all people; and that I will, to the best of my power, cause the peace to be kept and preserved and prevent all offences against people and property; and that while I continue to hold the said office I will to the best of my skill and knowledge discharge all the duties thereof faithfully according to law."

Public interpretation is a hurdle that certain public officials have tried to master. There has been a change with the general publics view of the police in just recent years. With the worldwide access and simplicity in public media sites, a general populace that was once dependent on mainstream filtered media, has a new faster outlet, for in some cases incriminating evidence. An incident can reach the four corners of the globe without government intervention, and can sway the opinion of the tax paying public. The general view and consensus, has somewhat changed from protected to paranoid.

Inner-city life.
A strong, and in some cases, a proven approach is employing a local policing system. As many local inner-city youths will give testament, a known policing or authoritative figure, would be more trusted and respected than an 'outside' or unknown authority. Someone called Chester Goodchild from Surrey will be more discriminating in his interpretation of a situation, than someone who's conditioned and familiar with known territory.

An example of right from wrong?
In the spring of 1985, a young football supporter followed his team for an away game. His intent was to be part of all that went along with being a young minded English football supporter in the 1980's, but with his own added agenda, violence. A bottle of ammonia and a small hammer were his chosen trusted tools. The journey with his friends that ensued was typical of any generation and that included no more than whistling at pretty girls, the petty mild-mannered teenage comments at those in his group and an over confident attitude. Upon arrival at their destination, the young minded fan and his agenda were met with malice and the welcoming committee; violence commenced and upon one particular confrontation, a knife was pulled and shoved in the direction of the visiting fan. Grabbing the knife in an attempt to defend himself, allowed him to pull one of his concealed weapons. Drawing back his arm so as to build up power, he slammed down on the knife holding teen, not content with the first blow he drew back

again, but on this attempt, he felt himself being pulled back by a stronger force. Turning around, the visiting fan was now faced with what must have been the local police, who he instantly recognised as the person pulling him off the fan he'd just struck. The problem being, in the process, the London fan had struck the policeman in the face with his hammer. This event cost the 15-year-old a beating, from what is estimated to be at least 3 additional police in a police van. The fact remains if you hit the O.B expect repercussions. The fan consciously knew his objective from the start, he had a premeditated orchestrated and a mindset focused on personal victimization. That journey home, was one of the most painful he'll not forget. It didn't stop him, but he remembered the cardinal rule; there's a price to pay when unjustifiably striking an authoritative figure.

An example of a questionable arrest?
Junior Palmer.

The following is a statement given by my surviving brother, James. Along with several other witnesses, they gave statements reflecting an accurate account of an assault by plain clothed (who didn't initially identify themselves as law enforcement) and uniformed police.

James Allday – "On 10th of September at 7:30 PM, I was standing outside my house talking to a friend that lives locally, when **** came around the corner, and joined the conversation. Then I noticed a Fiat bravo pull up at the side of my house, and the driver was talking on a walkie-talkie. **** proceeded to walk in the opposite direction of the car, then I saw another cop pulled up at the other end of my street blocking the remaining exit. Then **** ran into my house and the men from the pulled-up cars, jumped out and shouted "****, wait!" Then they entered my house and ran upstairs. So, I walked over to my front door, and my mom said "James go and watch them". So, I went upstairs and one of the officers was kicking my bathroom door in. Three more officers, plain clothed, came up my stairs and stood behind the other officers. My brother, Junior was already by the bathroom door. Eventually the officer kicked my bathroom door open, and then about 3 to 4 officers jumped on top of **** and took my bathroom sink off with them. Then one of the CID officers pushed me and I went through the wall. He then grabbed me by my collar, and threw me into my mum's bedroom. I got up, and went back into the landing area where they were. Now there was 8 or 9 officers, some in uniform and one of them was calling for backup. I turned to my right, and saw about three offices trying to restrain my brother Junior, one of the officers had his left arm around Junior's neck, and this same officer was repeatedly striking Junior in the back of his head with his walkie-talkie. At this point, I could also hear **** screaming "the water is burning me", and eventually after a few minutes of struggling they carried **** and Junior down the stairs, and placed them in the marked police vehicles, with everyone shouting, I looked to my right and saw the people who live on the corner shouting racial comments, and the police did nothing.

In addition, there was a total of 5 other statements given to the police, reflecting this same information, and in addition the excessive physical force administered by the police against Junior while he was handcuffed resulting in injuries. This was documented by Northwick Park & St Marks NHS A & E department.

A complaint and file were made with the PCA, the police complaints authority. This is an independent body, established by Parliament, to oversee complaints by members of the public against police officers. On April 30th 2001, they responded stating they had investigated the complaint, interviews were conducted and statements from the officers in question were taken. The conclusion given was that the crown prosecution service did not consider that there was enough evidence, to support criminal charges against any officer. In addition, the excessive amount of damaged caused by the police would not be compensated.

In an earlier letter from the representing solicitor on November 26th 1999, stated Junior had been found not guilty on two charges of assaulting the police, but found guilty of obstructing a police officer whilst in the course of duty. He was subsequently fined for this charge. In a simple person's mind, there are some obvious unanswered questions. By what measure and authority were the plain clothed police, given permission to enter without a warrant? What level of force was necessary, to detain the one person they wanted? And at what stage was excessive force and restraint deemed acceptable, whilst striking a handcuffed unwanted person in the process?

If any trust is to be given, then it needs to be earned by those claiming they are viewed negatively by the general public. If local authorities and the governing appointed public servants put in place, are to criticize the view point of the tax paying public, then its a shared belief by many people, that accountability needs to be across the board. Monarchs of past employed a system excluding themselves from law, known as 'dispensing power'. The dispensing power held, in essence, that the then Monarch, were permitted to free himself or anyone that he chose from the obligations of the law. I'd like to think we've progressed from this fourth power, and Marxist mentality.

Shortly after, Junior had another altercation with the police, resulting in heavy injuries, not long after this he was found dead, the verdict was suicide! A police inquiry was conducted at the request of our family. It was decided there was no reason other than that the loss of life was a sole decision of Junior's own making, but questions remain. There were too many red flags, including a hand-written message left on the wall that has always been questioned if it was Junior's handwriting. The manner in the supposed suicide, including questionable evidence and knowing my brother's personality, and to accept their claim of suicide, blatantly contradicts his plans on coming to join both myself and family in the USA.

Jason Allday

Death of a cultural icon. Smiley Culture

David Victor Emmanuel was born in 1963 and raised in Stockwell, South London. He was the son of Guyanese parents. He earned the nickname 'Smiley' early in his life as it was said he would ask girls for a smile in an attempt in chatting them up. Certainly, one of his early accredited personality traits that made him a likable person. Prior to his recording career he worked as a DJ with many of London's reggae sound systems, most often with one of London's most known being Saxon system. Here, smiley met and worked with a number of other reggae artists, including Maxi Priest, Papa Levi and Tippa Irie.

His first single "Cockney Translation" was a Jamaican's guide to the recognised and long standing traditional East End vocabulary. Giving reference to known, typical London names and using them in comparison to names within the Jamaican immigrant community. The style and quality brought as much a comedy emphasis as a rhythmic style that complimented the new English reggae scene. "Cockneys have names like Terry, Arfur and Del Boy. We have names like Winston, Lloyd and Leroy." The song mixed cockney dialect with London's version of Jamaican patois, translating between the two. The song's lyric was later used in some inner-city schools as an example of how immigration has affected the English language. Smiley Culture popularised the 'fast chat' style of dj-ing that had originated with Jamaican d-jays such as Ranking Joe, and was developed further by British reggae toasters, particularly those on the Saxon sound system such as Peter King.

Smiley had chart success with his single, "Police Officer", released in late 1984. This was the tale of how he was arrested for the possession of cannabis, but then let off in return for an autograph when the police officer recognised him as the reggae artist Smiley Culture. Contrary to the song highlighting the use of drugs, and more probable the fact that most upper middle class programming and heads of departments within the British radio stations in the 1980's were not familiar with terms such as "ganja" and "sinsemilla", the single was a Top 20 hit, and earned Emmanuel appearances on BBC Television's popular music programme, Top of the Pops. Even though the record complimented smiley's known comical side in chatting, it did have a serious message, in that it highlighted the way black people believed they were unfairly treated by the police in 1980's England. In December 1984, Smiley recorded a show on Janice Longs BBC show and continuing with his success in early 1985, was featured on the covers of some very notable and influential music magazines including Echoes, Record Mirror, and the NME. The success of "Police Officer" prompted a re-release of "Cockney Translation". It picked up a decent amount of airplay on national radio. His popularity and success led Smiley to an appearance at the Reggae Sunsplash festival in Jamaica in 1985.

In July 2010, smiley was arrested and charged with conspiracy to supply cocaine, he later appeared on the 28th of September at Croydon Magistrates' Court in London. On 15 March 2011, it is alleged by the arresting police that David Victor Emmanuel, died from a single self-inflicted stab wound, while the police were searching his house for class A drugs. The record showed that shortly after the police arrival with a search warrant, Smiley took his life with a knife, piercing his own heart. A police post-mortem examination revealed that he had died from a single stab wound to the heart. Smiley left a vacuum in the reggae scene yet to be filled. His mother, son, daughter, sister, three brothers and many tens of thousands of fans survive him.

Jason Allday

Smiley Culture will always be remembered as a major influence in the music industry, complimenting the hard working and creative Jamaican immigrants. There are some within the black music community that feel in addition to the creative and unique style he created, a bench mark was set by a pioneering gifted artist we all called smiley culture.

Asher Senator

"He who is compassionate to the cruel will ultimately become cruel to the compassionate"- Eliav Shochetman

When you share a passion and a platform for something you both enjoy doing, nothing can take that memory away, that's what makes that loss much harder to accept. They say music is the voice of your soul; the day Smiley was taken from us, and a part of me was unfairly taken too. I have questions, questions to this day that have not been answered. I question at the time of his death, the police report suggested that Emmanuel had stabbed himself while going to make a cup of tea in the kitchen of his Surrey home. That posed another simple question in itself, as Surely Smiley would have been handcuffed, as in normal practice during any raid as to prevent the suspect disposing of evidence, harming officers or himself. How is it that he managed to stab himself whilst in handcuffs and if not in handcuffs, why not?

Secondly how did he get hold of a knife when surrounded by police officers? He surely would have been closely monitored and guarded by police officers and an officer would have supervised his every move Even on the most basic of searches, a suspect is not left out of the officer's view. One report suggested he went into another room, again why unmonitored, and trusting the nature of the alleged claim of class A drugs being in smiley's house, why would smiley be left out of sight?

Thirdly how is it, if, as the police say, he stabbed himself, how is it he is surrounded by officers and yet they could not prevent him from doing so?

Finally, once he was injured, why could they not apply first aid and call for immediate medical assistance to save his life? What time did they arrive at the property and what time was the ambulance actually called?

I remember the day of what I thought would be justice for my friend, I remember following the rules and walking the line of fair trial and protocol, I remember the anger and hurt as I shouted out in court "you're killing us!" and I remember being pulled from the court. The cries of "no justice, no peace" were chanted by friends and family and many left the court in protest, the meeting was then adjourned. No one is making any unfair accusations, but there are more unanswered questions than answers. The fact remains that Smiley died under very questionable circumstances, I'm no lawyer and I'm not a policeman, but we all know that the police have a sworn duty to care for a suspect, regardless of their alleged crime. I believe the police failed to enforce and maintain simple protocol. The result was the loss of a gifted young man, the police system is a necessary part of our society, but losing innocent lives isn't!

When I think of my friend, I feel a great sense of pride, when I talk of him; it's with a great sense of respect and to think he had an influence on the highest chair in the country, as Smiley was invited to meet Her Royal Highness. She had commented she'd listened to his records in the palace. The single 'police officer' was based on a true story, and the value that smiley brought to our shared craft integrated cultures through music. A black youth talking cockney and gaining acceptance in a culture enriched in tradition, is a feet in itself. Smiley helped bridge that racial divide that existed, and society benefited from this.

If I was to speak for smiley, I know he'd say that he was a British icon, not just a black icon. He carried a philosophy that was bigger than just the colour of a man's skin. He was a proud, gifted and a liked individual and I miss my friend we all called Smiley Culture.

Killed or murdered? Was it an indiscriminate attack?

On April 1st 2009, PC Harwood killed Ian Tomlinson during a baton attack. As a result, Mr. Tomlinson died on the city street. An investigation led to a not guilty verdict on the manslaughter charge. Mr. Tomlinson, was pushed and then struck from behind by the PC as he walked away from a police line in the City of London during the G20 protests, he later collapsed and died. The last time a police officer was successfully prosecuted for the death of somebody in custody was in 1969, when two Police officers responsible for the death of David Oluwale, the first black man to die in police custody in the UK, were successfully prosecuted. This should have been a mile stone event, but to date, no police have been prosecuted, or convicted of the death of someone whilst in police custody.

Jason Allday

Paul King

"I'm only riding with who I walked with, and I'm only eating with those I've starved with"- Evelyn Lozada

There's always two sides to a story, always another opinion, always more than meets the eye and no truer than the injustice and the lies behind what would be known as the death of Ian Tomlinson. So, let me attempt at filling in the void, they so easily missed. On the morning of April 2nd 2009, I was staying at my mums, in my mind no different than any other day, mum was doing well that morning, considering there was typically 9 kids under foot, and that alone would send most parents to lose their minds and sanity. Around 6 am I was getting myself ready for work and I heard a knock at the front door, my initial thought was 'it's a bit bloody early!' two old bill from the city of London police, had turned up and presented, what they'd been told were the facts surrounding my dad's death. We were told, our dad had passed away and they thought it was a heart attack! This news struck all of us as hard as anyone could imagine. We all broke down; such a simple statement had an affect in an immeasurable way. They continued with what little 'facts' they had. They advised us, he'd got caught up in the riots that day, and as a result, he'd lost his life. How the fuck could someone lose their life, in something they had no involvement in? This wasn't a war-torn Bosnian high street; he was walking home from his London based newspaper stand, no different than any other day. The story just didn't sit right, not with me or anyone that could compose themselves enough to try and get their head around the story being presented to us. Over the coming week, we had police at our house and it would seem everywhere we went. To make things worse, mum could not see his body for about 6 days. Then of course we had to contend with the papers contacting us, telling us variations of the incident! To their credit, one mainstream newspaper presented compelling evidence contrary to what we were told by the London city police! What made the story being given to us by The Guardian newspaper more listenable, was wording that included police contact with my dad and discrepancies to the initial story. Added to the statement given by the Guardian was the fact there was video showing a uniformed police officer striking my late father, and as a result contributing, if not causing his death! In my mind, this was unquestionable incriminating evidence, and what we thought would help bring justice was the fact the officer could be identified! The fact there was video showing the cowardice act caught on video was better than an eyewitness, or so we thought!

Adding insult to injury, proving the world can be a truly cruel and heartless place, a member of the family didn't know of the death, they got the worst of news when they went to the shop that morning and got the Sun newspaper, only to see the photos of him already dead. There are no words, or way I can emphasis the pain and anger I felt. To see those closest around you being given the news that the one back bone of your family, someone that has always been there for you, is never going to be part of your lives again, to say it was killing us that day is an understatement. It just didn't seem real.

In the coming week, anger and hatred would find its way to me. We were told information, by what is supposed to be a trusted source and part of an infrastructure that is promoted and sold to us as a service. It's a demographic that is supposed to be part of our great country, that is in trusted to mold the common populace by laws of this country together. It's a recognisable department, that's there to promote civility amongst the common working men and women of this country. It's a part of what we see every day and they lied, they fucking lied to us! We were led to believe, dad had died of a heart attack. We were told it was due to a natural cause. We and the whole of the country were let down and treated with no respect. Even with the involvement of the I.P.C.C and a coroner, proved no more than a waste of time, broken promises and more misplaced trust. There will always more questions than answers, relating to the death of my dad, one of the most asked, is why was the mentioned policeman, working within the MET, after it was disclosed he had a very questionable past, within the very same police force!

Continuing with their total disregard for truth and our integrity, as proved later on, the police arranged for us to visit dad's football team. My initial thought was to try and accept that there may be decency within society. My thoughts were to try and lead by a positive example for my family, but my gut instinct was telling me to question their actions and intentions. Bit by bit, piece by piece, the truth and the actual events of that hateful day unfolded!

So where am I with all of this? Instead of a life long adventure, a boat load of banter, memories and experience with my dad, I'm left with emptiness and hate. The word hate, to some, is a word that if measured by its very meaning, is a reflection of the destructiveness that exists in the world. To some, it's a word that can be identified and attached to certain facets of society, it's also a word that can be thought of as part and parcel of the evil in a person's heart, to me, it's a word that filled a void, created by the lowest of the low. Hate is also a word where you'd like to try and forgive someone; the alternative is to hate them for the rest of your life. When my dad was killed, I wanted to hate everyone, but thought it would make my life hell. I didn't blame society as a whole, they're not to blame, but I knew and felt someone was. I then wanted to kill all the police or at minimum hurt them, much like they hurt me and those around me. Hate to me is a rage in the body that wants to get out, but also, not to let the wrong person get it. Initially that's why I held back, but like most living things, only so much can be suppressed, coerced or dealt with on a dignified level. From this point, I looked at it in a very simple way - was dignity applied to my father when a baton came down on him, changing our lives and the taking of his?

Looking at the role and importance of a father can be interpreted many ways. In biblical terms, it's said the role of a father. (Ephesians 6:4.) says there is no role in our modern society that suffers greater neglect, as far as God is concerned, than that of the father. In modern day society, it can be as much a physical benefit as a psychological one. It's certainly one that's open to debate and interpretation, except in my heart and mind - there was a moral obligation clearly shown, when I look at the relationship my dad invested in us all, and one he'd accomplished well.

To dad, he saw his responsibilities as less of a science, but more simply as one of ethics; he identified with his role. Rationality with his response and reasoning. That's why it makes it all that much harder with the bullshit surrounding his death! He wasn't morally superior in anyway, he always maintained a level of empathy, of course added with his charm and 'can-do attitude'. "You want to earn a few quid, well those dishes aren't gonna' clean themselves, Paul" philosophy. What makes it that much more with him, he was my step dad and, in his mind, we were his life and his children. He took on the arduous task of raising another man's children - and he fucking shone! It is an ambitious task, many men, who, if being honest, will tell you how difficult it is filling another man's shoes, all the while consciously accepting, even though the children aren't of his making, their care and welfare now is. He filled those shoes, and when I think of him, it's hard to think of anyone being any better. He was the person that would rather buy a copy of the big issue, than conform to the false ideals of certain registered charities, always doing 'his bit'. Much like myself, he despised those that would elevate themselves to a moral high ground, a 'holier than tho' type, as dad was all 'hard work', 'being true to your own' type of character'. With his flaws, warts and down to earth mannerism, there was nothing false about him.

Sometimes, it appears that there's a natural defense and high level of protection in place for the police, a 'they can't do wrong' attitude. Let's be honest, they're a paid service of the establishment, in place to provide and maintain law and order; but what they're not paid to be is an extreme fascist, hard core, right wing enforcer of a false narrative! We are supposed to live in a free and fair democracy. They're supposed to maintain a level of governed civility, the promise of shared indiscriminated protection, not to commit murder and then not be held accountable. It's become much easier for these events to occur and go unpunished. With more documented events of civil unrest and acts of violence in the world, I feel the governments boot-boys have declared war on the general public. An unprecedented amount of vicious attacks and deaths have been brought to the public's attention, but still no justification in fair and due process. You're supposed to celebrate indiscriminately with people you care for, not as a memory, not as a shadow of the past and certainly not because of how they were murdered. Sometimes, hate isn't a strong enough word. I'll push this opinion, as its one that needs to be understood and learned from. When you say Disney world, the first thing that comes to mind is Mickey Mouse. When you say the English seaside, you think of, and if you're lucky enough, you'll get a sunny day, sticks of rock and your family freezing their arses off in the sea. Now, when I think of the police, it invokes a memory and an empty chair where he once sat, a door he'd walk through and greet us all, and a memory the he was murdered, it really is a bitter sweet existence. If there's trouble or where someone is in need of protection, a person is supposed to be confident and safe in believing the boys in blue are only a simple phone call away, not, at what might be their demise.

The official acknowledgment of my dad's death is written and presented with so little care and concern, the lack of empathy shown in it is a crime. One report I read was as cold and callus, it again shows the ignorance with what really happened and the blanket story spun by mainstream. It read 'Ian Tomlinson, was a newspaper vendor who collapsed and died in the City of London after being struck by a police officer during the 2009 G-20 summit protests. A later inquest found that the officer, Simon Harwood, a constable with London's Metropolitan Police Service, had unlawfully killed him. Harwood was later found not guilty of manslaughter, but was dismissed from the police service for gross misconduct'. Once written, the incident, like many others, has been shelved and forgotten about. The lack of compassion and contempt doesn't reflect any justice, just the ignorance from up with our leaders and government.

So, the moral is for you to accept there's two sides to every story, to identify the enemy, which in this case is the untruths and show respect to people that sometimes don't deserve it. Remember, that by following their actions, makes you the same fool, be bigger and better. By these actions, you'll be a reflection of your own character and strength.

A soldier's story, a soldier's conflict

There's an obvious parallel with a boy and the military, maybe it's an instilled belief or tradition being born on an island – something that needed defending. Many identified with the failures and the success of military training, as many sports that we're exposed to through our young years, also instill a level of accomplishment and merit upon success. As a nation, we're raised to identify with a level of respect and discipline, being a soldier within H.R Highnesses military can certainly exemplify this trait. Some of our greatest leaders have come from a military background, for it was once said, that Sir Winston Churchill was born with a sense of destiny, I could add being of an island race, we're born with a sense of inheritance; born British, born proud. The military teaches you to be humble through humility. The military training can teach you success from failure; no candidate is 100% in their training

P.T.S.D

"You never get over it!" is a typical comment you'll hear or read with the subject relating to P.T.S.D. Post-traumatic stress disorder (PTSD) is an anxiety disorder that may develop after an individual is exposed to one or more traumatic events. The term is one that has only been widely accepted within the last decade; previous terms included shell shock, battle fatigue and soldiers' heart. People who experience assault-based trauma are more likely to develop PTSD, as opposed to people who experience non-assault-based trauma, such as witnessing a traumatic event. This invisible scaring and psychological damage can have not only a life long effect on the victim, but also their family. During war, military service members are exposed to a number of potentially traumatic events —they are not limited to an individual's life when it's in critical danger, but also when he or she is seriously injured, there is a threat to physical integrity, including others within their scope. In order to meet criteria for a diagnosis of PTSD, in addition to being exposed to at least one potentially traumatic event as already mentioned, an individual must react with helplessness, fear or horror either during or after the event. It is a subject that has had as many failures in treatment as success. Each and every person that fights P.T.S.D will tell you of their personal harrowing ordeal and reoccurring nightmares, but one fact is consistent with them all, it is an illness they all wish they could live without.

Simon Bywater

"In every man there is a soldier. Life will dictate the battlefield, you'll decide on the level of courage"- An unknown soldier

It wasn't something I'd considered as a young boy, you know, being a caped crusader or the action man type. I was your average young English boy, growing up, respecting my family, enjoying Christmas and holidays with them all, the usual stuff. I never thought about committing to the military until I witnessed the Falklands conflict on TV, that day changed me and would start me on a course that would dictate the rest of my life. My start in the military, like most, was the recruitment process. The rig moral was something I'm sure most would agree was tedious and lengthy, but a necessary process. You could get a sense of pride being shown by the recruiter in his presentation and promoting of the service, a person that would still carry the flag into an earth scorched battle scenario, a fully loaded weapon and the hardened experience from his time in the field, well, it's how I thought of it. I like to think that reality through experience is a practice earned and the British Marines was what I wanted to become part of; a specialist group of people, trained to be without question, one of the most recognised and formidable services in the world. When I told my family, there wasn't the enthusiasm I'd expected, this then only made me want to accomplish the training and pass the near impossible even more, not then to say 'I told you so', but to get the encouragement and support I'd hoped to get from them in the beginning.

Jason Allday

The written test and the introduction to the training was at the recruitment centre, this much like the time signing up passed quickly. Before I knew it, I was on my way to complete and in my mind pass the potential Recruits Course (PRC) at Lympstone Commando Centre (CTCRM) in Devon. This is the part where they see if you 'have what it takes', putting applicants through physical and mental agility testing. Before I knew it, I was covered in mud, crawling around an assault course, attempting to master a gym, maneuvering around narrow Devon country lanes and swimming in various types of clothing. There wasn't much breathing or relaxing time during the three-day trials. The news from a cold faced, unemotional recruitment sergeant voiced what I wanted to hear. I was in, I'd passed! My first trophies accompanied me home in the shapes of blisters and abrasions, all part of the experience. The 23rd of September 1985, I received my orders via the post, but my parents still failed to show the enthusiasm I'd hoped for. On my day of departure, seeing me off at the train station, I had my one-way ticket to full fill my new ambition and become part of the British Royal Marine Commandos. Did I honestly think I'd earn the right to wear the Green Beret? I was going to fight until I did! My family from here on was troop 296. Cold, exhausting and both mentally and physically exhausting, that was commando training. It was never easy, there was not one day or night I regretted or questioned joining, there wasn't one step of either my left or right foot that didn't experience pain and torment from the floor below. There wasn't a part of my physical or mental being that didn't experience pain. Until you've experienced the hell that a recruit goes through, you'll never be able to feel the pride and accomplishment the successful recruit carries with him, that feeling he carries for his whole life, when he gets to don the Green Beret. Each meal I got to eat, every minute of sleep, a day there was a sign of a moments reprise were something I'd not truly appreciated until I'd gone through training. For me, commitment was felt when I signed a nine-year contract, for me the pride was being known as part of the Kings Squad.

Being on a NATO exercise is much like going into a restaurant, being presented with a menu in every other language than what you are familiar with and being entrusted to order a meal that'll you enjoy or understand what it is you're eating. One thing remains true, a soldier is a soldier, the training will dictate the type of soldier, there is a difference in a person's exposure to various types of arms but when you're faced with the decision of saving and preserving a human's life, you're all the same. Flesh and bones feel and react the same to bullets and mortars. I had the pleasure of being around some real soldiers, who had heart and soul and without a second would've put down for those in the fight. Politics is everywhere, including the military, it's in some parts of the military more than others, and as I experienced, in some countries armed forces more than others. Politics and the military conflicts, as does politics with most things in the real world, so know your equipment, know your weapon and be there for those around you, simple!

The hardest thing to let go, and in some cases it's a curse, is the 'human element' that you experience when 'in field'. When you're on the other side of the world, and a friend is in a near death situation, your local E.R isn't going to be an option. Whilst in the jungles of Brunei, I was with a group of men, that deserved all the happiness and success you could wish for. A friend I served with, was one of those. Watching a friend on the brink of death, watching a man drift in and out of consciousness, the cold clammy feel from his body, the chance of losing some one so far from home was an easy option, but not one we'd allow. Although I never saw him again, the man he was and the strength he always showed, I know he is on top of the world. This experience wasn't the first of mental scaring a marine will carry, and as time showed I was to experience a lot more.

Being sent to war is a battle all in itself. There's no amount of mental preparation that can ready you for this. One minute you're planning a future with someone, the next you're saying goodbye, knowing full well the reality of war. The statistics in war time casualties are something you may or may not know, your success in coming home is another guarantee you're not promised, and when you glance at the faces in the same armoured carrier as yourself, it's a historical fact that some of these boys will never come home again. The dependency and reliance of your discipline is something you owe not only to yourself but also the men you are sworn to work with. There's a motto known between many factions, one I know and have lived by, is preserve and protect mine and those around me. When you're heading towards a conflict, you have to carry the hardships you learned in training, you have to carry on, you have to fight for what you know is right. Operation Desert Storm was to me part of my life, a time that instilled memories, both good and bad. It was code named Operation Desert Storm in its combat phase, and was a war waged by coalition forces from over 30 nations, led by the United States against Iraq in response to Iraq's invasion of Kuwait. I was honest to myself from the start, there are always casualties from any war; some justified some not, but all the same, those that entered the war do so for a reason. Mine was due to watching the Falklands conflict many years ago on a black and white TV, mine was to serve and serve proudly and it was here I would carry myself with full honour and pride. Traveling to the start of the battle was via a C130, a beast of a machine that got the job done. It was within the first 24 hours, that I started to realise I was on the other side of the world. Many people back home would be worrying about their journeys home through traffic or the catching the start of a TV show. My reality was to protect their lives and those I cared for.

Our base camp was just outside the most northern part of Iraq. We had to enter via a manned Turkish control point, the nearest town was called Salopi, the town was represented by the sounding of its name; something that needed a good hosing down and a fresh start, something these poor souls would never see. The day light hours allowed the few westerners that may have visited that part of the world a glimpse of basic supplies and same wares from one store to the next. The night-time produced a different type of resident. With political turmoil in place, the conflict in Northern Ireland is as close a parallel as I can relate to. Terrorist operations against the Turkish military were commonplace. The time came for our unit to move into northern Iraq and my life to become part of military conflict and history. The small amount of buildings remotely scattered around bore the scars of a war-torn conflict. Expressionless border guards occupied a number of check points we passed, I can only guess the months they'd been here had taken an effect on their morale and lack of motivation. We eventually crossed over the river Khabur and were now officially in enemy territory. The sound emitted from the tires on our land rover against the tarmac was the only audible noise; an eerie quietness reminded me to aim the 50-caliber gun at any potential problems. The only time you'd know there was a problem would be when you were taking enemy fire, and then, it could be too late. The terrain produced so many textbook examples of an ambush or hidden enemy combatants. We arrived near an area known as Zakho, and it was here a sight is one that is etched in my memory forever. The first casualties of war are always the innocent lives, and there is none more innocent than a child. Upon entering the area, we observed young children playing; you'd expect not to be any different than any other child of their age. The innocence in children is a precious thing, what wasn't were the lives these children lead. Their ragged clothed bodies enjoyed each other's company; their mud-dried hair hadn't seen one of the most precious commodities in this part of the world, water, in months. The gutter and the dusty road was their playground. Passing the children, you couldn't but help notice their dusty faces, some encrusted with flies and dirt from the road they played in. One young girl caught my attention standing in the roadside as we slowly passed, her once blue dress was covered in dried mud and in tatters. Handing her some boiled sweets from my rations, she clutched on to them as if her life depended on them. To my horror, I noticed in her other hand she was holding on to an anti-personal mine. This young innocent life literally had both hers and my life in her hand. You'd only expect to see a child holding onto a doll or a stuffed toy, not something that could destroy two lives. The scene escalated even worse as the minutes passed, the bargaining for the mine from the young girl, prompted scores of other children to rush towards us with their own bargaining chips. More anti-personal mines, RPG rocket heads, AK-47 assault rifle bayonets and assortments of ammunition. Our path was a simple one, and that was to leave as quickly as possible. We continued to our rendezvous point, this was a town occupied by the coalition and Kurdish forces.

Working in isolated locations has a psychological effect on a person. The invisible dangers including snipers, mines and potential ambushes all take their toll. The proficiency and skill I'd learned as a British commando, is training that without question saved my life in all aspects of the war. There's nothing more reckless than seeing the loss of life due to poor training and bad leadership decisions. Sharing a war with a contingent of Kurdish guerrilla fighters in an open back truck and witnessing them hurtle out of control, causing a loss of lives, shows the reason and justification in the back breaking, soul testing training the forces receive. It makes you think how many casualties of war there is due to these moronic incidents. My deployment ended and I received my orders to return home, not before I witnessed more carelessness that affects lives over carelessness and lack of professionalism; a soldier's job is one that requires discipline and above all dedication.

Back in England, my time in Iraq felt a million miles away and I'd hoped it would become something I could be proud I was part of. The feeling of coming home from the conflict and the violent environment, to a life with my wife and the safety and security was now in motion. The next step was to simply settle into a new job and allow nature and fate take its course. There were very few careers that I could identify with and the most obvious was the police force. Structure, discipline and job security was how I read the position. Training, exams and a few interviews and I'd bagged the position. Greater Manchester police force was now to be my 'nine to five'. There was plenty of work for an able bodied young person like myself, and there was no shortage of enthusiasm on my part. What should have been an easy transition back into civilian life and a job that I predicted would be on par with the marines, was to say the least frustrating and a big let down. The work was there, Manchester, known as 'gun-chester' to mainstream media and criminals, was the work load any one wishing to be of service, but what was missing was the support from the higher ups. Budgets, the over politicisation of the police force and their practice and literally, a wrapped in cotton wool philosophy and attitude started to impede what should have been the necessary strength needed in a government body. Grown men winging about the most miniscule items, heightened sensitivities and a lack of upper management knowledge on real street practices further restricted the necessary approach needed for any of us that cared to get the job done. There were some good people to work with, but I know I wasn't alone in my thoughts on what was wrong and made things unnecessarily difficult. I knuckled down, made the effort and worked hard. I was part of a team that covered the largest inner-city council estate in Europe, Wythenshawe. No shortage of work and plenty of opportunities to make a go of things.

My first child was born, I was working hard and enjoying my civilian life (a few frustrations with work, but I was the get the job done type) so, life was slowly coming together. Working nights was always the biggest challenge, accepting life isn't meant to be easy, I mustered the effort necessary, but even with the effort and good people to rely on, the little or no back up, lack of resources and the over stretched budgets, that always seemed to dictate more importantly than the security and safety of not only ourselves but the general public started to wear on me. My next child came along, and I was as happy as I could wish for with my family. It was here, seeing the most precious thing in my life, my children, I started to realise the environments I'd been exposed to. The little girl in Iraq and those poor souls, thousands of miles away, unprotected and god only knows their fate. Why did I feel guilty? I've worked hard; played by the rules and here I am thinking about the welfare of people I'll never see again.

Work was now recording violent crime after violent crime, with each day passing, the stabbings, violent assaults and crimes all just started to blend into one big haze. It was never ending. My personal life started to make an unpredicted change too. Going out for a social drink would typically include a comment of 'oh, he's a copper'. You could notice a change in people's tone and conversation; there was no social time with anyone that was outside of the police force. Friends and family were a select few, but life was becoming a bit harder than I felt was fair.

One of the most unforgettable experiences I witnessed happened after we received a call to respond to a disturbance outside a pub. It was reported that a group of men had been seen fighting, the time was shortly before 11 pm. Racing to the scene we pulled up to be met by other responding officers and a divisional K-9 unit. Upon reviewing the area, there was no one to be seen and warranted a call to confirm the location. Upon returning to our vehicle and scouting the area, we were waved down by a member of the public and advised of the location of a person that was lying in the near by bush. Upon closer examination it was evident this person had sustained some serious injuries, as walking towards him, I noticed what should've been dry grass was actually very wet, but I was horrified to discover it was his blood. The victim frantically tried to get up, his clothes were soaking with blood from his injuries. I needed to help; I needed to keep this man alive. "What's your name?" I asked, he replied, "I'm in the army, home on leave, a group of kids jumped me". Very quickly the victim become aware of the extent of his injuries and attempted to move. In desperation, I think he just wanted to just get away from the incident, maybe a way in removing himself from the whole situation. Instinctively I told him to lie down and relax and help is on the way. I was franticly calling over the radio for an ambulance. The victim started to cry; he was fighting hard, telling me he was going to die if we didn't get him to a hospital. His voice started to get quieter; I had to move closer to his face to hear him. In front of me I saw the life drain from his eyes. His eyes started to dilate and roll back in his head. The words become softer and more desperate, "get my mum, I want my mum". I couldn't let him go, I refused to let this man go, this was my responsibility, my job. I looked into his eyes as he slipped in and out of consciousness. "Stay awake, do not fall asleep!" I screamed at him. He'd lost a lot of blood; his pulse was very week and I struggled to find it. There were a number of stab wounds over his body including his legs and stomach. Looking back into his eyes, I repeated his name in an attempt to keep him conscious but as he looked at me I slowly watched him begin to die. "Where's the fucking ambulance?" I shouted, the victim was hanging onto me as I knelt over him, his grip weakening with each breath and second that passed. "Where's the fucking ambulance, where's the fucking ambulance?" I kept screaming. This man was dying in my arms, I was powerless, and all I could do was sit there. Politics and procedure restricted my helping this man any further, fucking politics again! This isn't me, I need to save this mans life, was my only thought. Bollocks, I need to do something. I was of the mindset that I would move and try and save this man's life, my conscience demanded that. I told the supporting police officers we'd be taking the man directly to the A & E ourselves and they all agreed. Whilst doing this, I needed to make sure the victim was still with us, he was still breathing, I needed to save this man. I soon realised my worst fear, he'd stopped breathing. I attempted mouth to mouth but I'd lost him. The paramedics arrived at this moment moving into action and got the victim onto the ambulance, but even with their skill and experience there was no bringing back the young man. Upon arrival at the A & E, I got out of the ambulance feeling numb and empty, only a few hours before, this young man was thinking of nothing but going out for the night, and what the rest of the week may bring. I felt a pain and void were there was once a stronger man, but knew this was part of the job and tried to bury what had just happened in the back of my mind. Walking into the hospital, I was suddenly surrounded by people shouting hysterically, asking what had happened and asking countless questions. I was in a haze; everything around me was a blur. I couldn't find the answers they needed on the young man that had just died in my arms. The words "I'm his mum" awakened me from my daze, then asking me what happened. The life line and by no underestimation the backbone of every hospital are the nurses, they are angels in a service that goes largely unappreciated and forgotten in this country. It was one of these angels that stepped in and took control, leading the relatives to a separate room so their questions could be answered. "How is my son?" was a question I didn't know how to answer. I still believed the staff at the A & E would bring him around. All I could do was regain a level of professionalism, stand straight and say their son was in a serious condition and excuse myself. It was here a hospital consultant advised me the young man was dead. This I already knew, and it still just didn't sit with me. The hardest part was feeling helpless when he died in front of me, years as a professional soldier, one of the best outfits in the world and I lost him. I couldn't save him, so what words could I offer to comfort a family who had lost a son? The words I couldn't recall if I was asked, but the feeling is one that remained with me. A feeling of the deepest sadness isn't even close. I remember all I could do was comfort them. How do you tell someone his or her son has been murdered? I had become emotionless, I was now mentally drained. I entered into a different division of the police force, hoping this would send me both mentally and physically in a different direction. An opportunity was via a phone call to join the CID in the Moss side area. It was far from appealing to your average Joe, but being an ex marine, I felt I was suited for the position. Moss Side was the gangland area of south Manchester. It's large multi cultural community consisting of Afro Caribbean's, Africans, Asians, Whites and as many others was as close to other known areas with their own acts of violence and problems around the world. In each and every incident I dealt with, there was one consistent truth, anyone and everyone was a target for the animals that committed these unspeakable crimes. Here, I started to realise that I was once a soldier defending the lives and best interests of these people and I'd now myself become a target. The conflict in me was starting to identify itself as a big problem in my personal life. The conflict was reinforced by outside forces; the general public viewed me as an enemy. Those that were the victims, were the only ones that could save themselves raised the barriers, but they never wanted to talk. Their animosity and the powers I reported to become all too much. I was dealing with the night I lost Robert all over again, every day and every minute. I was drowning, there was only one person that could change this and help me get out of this endless battle, and it was myself. The final call was in 1997, when a visiting student was stabbed to death. The accused had taken a life over some cash and a single gold ring. A visiting student, who was studying at Manchester University, only trying to better his life by investing in an education. He was of no threat to anyone and his only crime was walking through a park one evening. He died as a result of two stab wounds. He bravely staggered out of the park where he was attacked onto a busy road, where he then collapsed. His attackers had left him for dead. Some honourable people rushed to his aid, but despite the efforts of the local A & E department, the student died from his injuries. I was part of the investigative team that was responsible for the dealing of the murder case and was joined by some quality people in getting the case finished, and even though the main accused attacker walked from that charge, he was later arrested and convicted of both that murder and another charge that included a very nasty aggravated rape at knifepoint charge.

The constraints and the other overwhelming issues within the police department, made me question more than ever if I was still the person I was joining the force. Here I was in one of the most violent places in Europe, where teenagers are as armed as some militias in third world countries and I'm being told about the importance of underlining segments of my journal. I began to hate my job, I began to get frustrated over everything in a system that was supposed to be my savior, I started to dislike and find fault in everything I tried to fix, and all I wanted to do to save a populace my family was living amongst. Whilst investigating serious violence and murder, I realised there is a fine line between life and death. The violence was in many cases resulting from very trivial matters. A man found with the kitchen knife in his head had died as a result of an argument over the sale of a weights bench. In another case a young man had a chisel forced into his skull during an altercation over a girl on the way home from a pub. It was all senseless and all I could do was bottle up my thoughts about these animals who committed these crimes. I certainly had no sympathy for them, or their pathetic acts. Deep down, I knew there was a problem, I felt a change and a feeling of desperation that needed addressing, but a soldier never folds, a man doesn't bend under a testing of his metal, I didn't want to appear weak. Another move, a new house and a change of scenery was the action I felt would cure this, I was wrong. The same feeling and anxiety followed me to work and home again. I couldn't find myself issuing someone a traffic ticket, there were people dying every day from the most pointless acts of violence, and who was I to impede on someone's right to earn a living? In a more relaxed town and work environment, I was given more time to reflect on my past. Here I started to find a place to search some meaning and understanding of my anger and frustration, it was here that I realised I was suffering with PTSD. I made steps in seeking professional help with my suffering and sought out counseling. It was one of the hardest and toughest hurdles I've ever approached. The necessary steps and treatment was a part of my life that saved me. I wasn't alone with this pain, it isn't something anyone ever has to feel is a sign of weakness and it is one of the bravest things I'd say I've ever accomplished. I left part of my life behind, and there are times I hold a level of resentment towards the police force. Their failure to identify the constraints of a necessary part of society, marred by budgets and the best interests of the upper management, they should know that those walking the streets are hampered by their lack of understanding for their safety and it's those officers that keep order in a violent and unforgiving world. I salute anyone man or woman that takes an oath to serve in the armed forces, you are heroes to many and saviors to us all. The British Royal Marines Commandos remains one of the highest respected services in my mind, and if I was to say if there is a necessary building block in any young boys' life, the services will make you a man and proud.

Jason Allday

Toastmaster

When early childhood intervention programs were initially introduced in the 1960's, its main goal was to increase the academic level of the identified child. But questions remained, what if a child slipped through the net, what would happen if it weren't until later in life, issues relating to social harms would be identified? There's a million 'ifs' and not always enough conclusions in today's ever-growing society. Most people working within the government complex, that has a child's best interest at heart, will tell you of as many success stories as losses. The world is a harsh and unforgiving one and no one, is as an easier target than a child.

There are also other ways children are saved from many a harsh environment and spiteful world, and some systems are as old as the issues themselves. Some of the biggest and most prominent achievers have been born from such situations and environments, but typically at a cost, and paid No more than the person affected by the experience. Every child deserves the experience of a caring family and a sanctuary within the home they grew up in. Some are granted neither, but as mentioned there is hope for some to be given a chance.

Society demands a consistent norm, and what is accepted by those around us, can ultimately play a deciding factor in the health and happiness in a person's life. Here the story starts with a young mother and her child in 1960's London. What ever the ultimate deciding motive may have been, a young boy was to part from his maternal mum. Thankfully there was a chance for this new born. Dr Banardos is part of a system that successfully connected someone in need, to someone that cares. A child isn't given the choice of his or her parents. Thankfully someone was willing to make that healthy choice for them. A child needs more than a fare chance. By today's standards, the issue and threat is very much evident. In recent reports its been suggested that teen violence has actually decreased, a good sign for over policed and over stretched budgets and better news for those that are at the most impressionable part of their lives. So, with everything going against some in their early lives, the safety net has been reinforced (but still not perfect). Whether it is at a child's initial start in this world, or later on in their young lives, more needs to be done to increase a child and young persons right to health and happiness. With life comes challenges, and many can be overcome by a person's efforts and continuing investment in their wish to succeed.

Jason Allday

Lennie Payne

"We all subscribe to a forum"- Anon

I was born on the 10th of April 1964 in Hammersmith, London, and named Mark Andrew Lewis. I was adopted at a very young age, so I have, as you would expect no memories of either parents. My mothers name was Pauline Georgina Lewis, once a resident in Kensington, London. I accept that some mothers are given the path of mother hood and mine chose another. It wasn't until I was in my mid twenties that I plucked up the courage to visit her, or rather locate via the only lead available. I had found her under 'mothers address' from my adoption certificate. I took my trusted pal Pugsy; a white boxer along for the visit. It was on this visit I also discovered it was once a hostel for unmarried mothers in the 1960's, that made a lot of sense I thought, and that was the last time I looked. My father was unknown, as my birth certificate has no mention of him. I've been told that 's how it was in those days.

My Adoptive parents, who I'm lucky, or to say more accurately, I was more blessed, had chosen me. Joan Irene Payne from Middlesex, and Leonard Walter Payne from Plaistow, East London, were to give me a loving home. We lived in Cranham gardens Cranham, Upminster in Essex. From memory, it was a nice area and worked well for a lot of people, being it was easily assessable from the city by the District line. My dad had bought a two-bed semi from new in 1960, for £1,800, leaving a hefty 25% down payment from the sale of his brand-new Ford car. Later, Dad and Granddad

Alan, acquired a couple more meters and built a double story extension, as the 12/10 ft. bedroom we all shared was getting a bit cramped. My mother loved children, but couldn't conceive, so they fostered through Dr. Barnardo's - they cared for many children over the years before adopting Andrew and then myself, then suddenly found out, she was pregnant with Gill, later came Stephen.

She had noticed when I had just started to walk, that I seemed a little off balance and kept walking into things. So, after a few bumps and falls, mum made an appointment with the Great Ormond Street Hospital. The out come was scoliosis (curvature of the spine) and a visit annually to Holborn to see if it got any worse. My earliest memories of visiting the hospital include a massive rocking horse in the lobby, the Queens square gardens, where we had our sandwiches and Alan's Magicians shop. I remember feeding the pigeons and also witnessing the most deformed and terribly handicapped children. I've never forgotten how more fortunate I was than some of those poor souls. They'd not even started their lives, and had already been horrendously cheated of a 'normal' or more fare existence. To this day, in my mind with regards to any humanitarian hardships, nothing stands equivalent than the statement 'health is wealth', as it was those memories that were to help give me strength in my later teens. When I was two, I had badly bloodshot eyes after walking into furniture, so my mother took me to the opticians, where they found me severely short sited. It was here I was to be awarded my first national health specs (another minor disability diagnosed!). I laugh now thinking 'mum, you can 'arf pick 'em', but I was one of her children, and she cared for me greatly.

A universal truth, is children can be quite cruel and spiteful and with four eyes and a twisted spine, I'd already got used to comments like Joe Ninety and the Milky Bar Kid - additionally, to add to the insults, a whole host of other suitable piss takes were later added. When I was about six or seven, a level of spitefulness was introduced, that quite frankly took me by surprise. The name-calling continued, but now with some comments I'd not yet experienced or heard. "You don't have a mum or dad"! This along with other snide and cold names, that sent my already suffering low esteem, to a whole new low level, that simply left me empty. My being brought into the world, had already made me question the unfairness that existed, but this new level of cruelty made me adopt even more self-doubt and questions. One level of questioning to myself was 'what do they mean?'. It resulted in my adoptive parents telling me the truth about my adoption. This bullying was the start of what became a big chip on my shoulder. They of course sat me down and explained the best they could, but eventually my parents and I decided to leave that subject alone for a few years. What my adoptive parents concentrated on was providing a warm and protective home. Something every child should be given and as a result of their commitment and hard work, I have lovely memories, that without question always make me appreciative of my adoptive family's kindness, and those include my grandparents on mum's side.

    After one particular week of bullying at school, my grandfather decided he'd step in and give me that guidance and support, he knew he could provide. I remember having a wonderful week when I stayed with my Nan and Granddad. My grandfather Alan was a very strict, but caring sort of man, they lived in leafy Stanmore in Middlesex. This one particular week, he took me everywhere. He showed me the whole of London, the Tower of London, Buckingham Palace, Nelsons column, Tower-Bridge, and the London history museum. During this visit, my granddad did, as most granddads would do, sat me down and become the pillar of strength and experience I needed. With a sprinkling of love and just enough 'old school' pep talk with regards to the adoption situation, would prove to be a great and much appreciated lesson for me in my young life. That visit allowed me to regain my belief, that there was care and understanding in my world. He truly was a great man and I'd go as far to say one of my childhood heroes. We also did an away day to the Isle of White with a coach full of old age pensioners, stopping every hour for a pee and a cuppa'. It's memories like these that make me think how lucky I was, but how cruel the world can be. They were great grandparents and I still think of them regularly. I can't go on without mentioning my auntie Flo and Uncle Jim, who lived down stairs from us, and who I loved to go and see. I remember they had just hand painted the kitchen furniture, the old vintage kitchen cupboards and left globules of paint underneath, which, for an unknown reason, I loved, and would feel the edges every time I went there and sat next to them. For me, it was the catalyst of my first experience with dripping paint and a lasting impressionism for future reference. Thinking back, it could be suggested it was an artistic experiment in art, I suppose something had stirred in me, or maybe it was an escape from everything that was going on at the time. Uncle Jim would always shake your hand in that ever so cripplingly tight way, which me and my brother's sister all hated.

My mother was a very strong lady, who had inherited her parent's strictness. "If you don't eat your dinner, you'll be eating it on the back step before you come back in", and not forgetting "off to bed without any tea" mentality! She was a proper mum though, who later ran the Moor Lane Chapel Nursery, where we all went every Sunday Religiously. We learned about Jesus and how 'he loved all the little children of the world', you know the song! Andrew and I went on to attend Jucos and Covenants, a kind of cubs and Scouts, (which we also did) where we got much deeper into the bible and its supposed meanings? 'For whoever believes in me, will inherit eternal life', more songs and dance! One day, the better side of my childhood curiosity came out and I asked the teacher, "So, do you have to be a Christian?". I remember previously thinking to myself, 'if you weren't born into a Christian family, then you didn't have a chance'! Didn't seem very fair, with 'all the children from the world' song. It made me very despondent to all these wise words. "You'll understand as God works in mysterious ways", was the teacher's reply. He was right there, as some years later he was banged up for noncing his own kids! What the fucks that about? I got a bit side stepped there, but again, something 'religiously' I supposed started to grow, be it a journey within, that had to be answered.

My Dad was an Engineering Pattern Maker, who worked at Fords in Dagenham. He was a lovely man, who's commitment to ensure we never went without, included his dedication to working every Sunday morning, (he said it was nothing to do with getting out of church) and the fact he took all that 'church business' with a pinch of salt. I remember He'd take us to Shoeburyness on a Sunday afternoon. We had our holidays at a friend's caravan in Dover court, Harwich. We would go every year in dads Ford Cortina and visit some other lovely places as a family. Holidays were fantastic as a kid, I absolutely loved them, we didn't have a lot, and looking back nobody did. French cricket; you didn't have a stump, one armed bandits, (smashed my teeth out on one of them), football, sea, sand, flying your first kite, picnics, and let's not forget the bench bike; if you don't remember it was two on the front, two on the back and off around the camp site, shrimping was a favorite. We would walk for miles, picking blackberries or gooseberries for dads home made wines or mums grumbles, absolutely wicked memories.

Dad was a real fitness fanatic, as a kid he was a gymnast. He even road a bike to France with his brother Ernie. Dad always included us in any of his pranks and adventures. He showed us how to head stand, back flip and swim. He loved to play football and show us how to tackle and coming from Plaistow, he was West Ham through and through. My Nanny Payne was an absolute Gem; she was a real old East End character. Her and Doris, my dad's sister, lived in Croydon rd. I loved it there, hammers this, West Ham that. Uncle Ernie and Maureen, Rob and Lynne, also used to come around and there was always an excitement in the air with their presence. With the banter and closeness, it was made to feel like a real authentic family, never harshness or malice, just real genuine people that cared for each other. They all talked a way that made it fun. 'Gawd blimey!' and 'Put the Kettle On will ya!' It was a time when you left your keys in the front doors, toilets out the back and all part of what I called my fun filled childhood. Your old two up two down houses, now these were old, but real interesting houses. The type with no front garden, us kids kicking a football about in the road! Yeah, no health and safety just good old plain football with the boys! (A far cry from the over commercialised game it is today). My mum hated it, I loved it! And we always had Fish and Chips in the daily rag.

I was always encouraged to draw by Nanny Payne, and I remember on one occasion, my dad bought me a book called 'So you want to know How to Draw'. It came with a full set of pencils that comprised of 6h to 6b, which he'd acquired or borrowed from Fords (he was reprimanded by mum for saying nicked, as this wasn't considered appropriate for children's ears) I was good at this and soon mastered each stage. Later on, I found out my paternal father had been an artist, and I wondered if he had recognised this talent in me or was it he was just a bloody all-round good Dad? Not saying my Mum wasn't but we had our issues, or being truthful, I probably had more. Growing up and looking back she did everything for the family and there were four of us. It just seemed I was forever being reprimanded by one of them, which made me feel suppressed by one and stimulated and encouraged by another, this was by my own interpretation your bad cop good cop schooling.

My invested time at school was as predicted, (mostly) a positive one. Hall Mead secondary school in Upminster Essex, was what I'd consider my start in art. Looking back I've often said they were the best and easiest years of my young adult life and rightly so. Not to sound the stereo typical old geezer, but school is without question a stroll in the park, my young friends. My school reports were generally good, although I got into a great crowd, resulting in regular canning by the headmaster. For those going through school now, the cane was a form of discipline that hurt and kept you in line. My wrong doings at school was for nothing more than cheekiness and mild disruptive behavior. My natural abilities allowed me to shine in art, which is where most of the teachers put me as a kind of solitary confinement, away from the more studious of the classroom attendees.

I was about 15 years of age, when a classroom fight in the art room ended with myself going into uncontrollable bodily convulsions. As a result, I was rushed to the hospital. The outcome was me being diagnosed as an epileptic, and this was my introduction to the frightening and unforgiving world of epilepsy. The process started with me having this jolt like shock down my right-hand side then with a massive rush of adrenalin, your body goes rigid and you hit the deck and shake, whilst you smash you nut into the floor. Yeah, lovely!! So, back to the quacks I go!

What do you get if you cross a blind epileptic with scoliosis? It's a Fuck off and Die you cunts experience!! To anyone unfamiliar to epilepsy, it's not just the rug being dragged out from under your feet, it's the room you're standing in being turned upside down, inside out and the lights being switched off. All the while, you lose every natural ability to maintain any of your senses, or will to hold your own. Coming around isn't any less comfortable. What was around you before the seizure and fit, has now changed immensely. It's like waking up in a foreign land without any knowledge of how or why you're there. And just to add a sprinkling of pain and disaster to your life, you have typically sustained injuries in the process. The majority of epileptic seizures are controlled by medication, particularly anticonvulsant drugs.

Phenytoin 100 mg daily

I'd left school and gained a place at Southend College of Arts, which I loved. I studied all aspects of art; still life, photography Art history the works. Of course, I had to touch and carry with me my child like attitude during college, and with my pals at the time, we had a laugh. Dave Gahan and his band Depeche Mode were doing lunchtime gigs and a few spliffs were past around, all superb times and it was here I'd experienced my first buzz (or second if you count spinning around and falling over disorientated as a kid). I had amazing afternoons in art lessons. On one occasion they included flicking rubbers at the nude's bums and having an uncontrollable laughing fit. Now artists and musicians in some respects share similar passions and interpret things very similarly, and the drug scene fits nicely into that equation. A whole cultural scene just kind of erupted and I was there, people's lives were taking off, there were opportunities clearly available but for the first time, I noticed I started to become two different people in side of me

Phenytoin 400 mg daily

Unbeknown to me, my life was about to take a roller coaster of a ride. I Dropped out of college, partly because of the increase of seizures on the trains and at the campus, plus the fact I was always skint. Art equipment cost a lot of money, and it wasn't free. It seemed then, that life was very unfair to me - drawing, painting and art were my passion, and it didn't seem to matter whether I followed the regime of anticonvulsants or not, nothing changed. Also, at the time, I felt there was a whole lot of fun to be had on drugs, and sometimes, I felt it was less pressure, or it was releasing the unwelcomed pressure. Deep down I was struggling with seizures, classes and everything else that was going on around me. Somethings you kept to yourself, but I should have opened up to my parents more and let them know, as well as everyone else, who thought that I was hard as oboes, of my struggle. Late nights, no money and a bad attitude was the point where

Lessons

I was shown the door, I was a little over 17. I remember my parting comment, "thanks Mum, just what I needed right now"

I Spent 6 nights with a mate called Simon, in a battered old Rover outside my mate Beaky's (RIP) flat, on the Cranham estate. We would stop the milkman every morning for a pint, and then we'd have it round the bakers in the morning, where they'd made a delivery before the shop opened. It wasn't the best, but we got through. Now nothing to do all day but get up to mischief, I started to think, what was I accomplishing? This was how it was for months. I needed a job, and I'd pretty much do anything, both legally and illegally. I'd had a sort of primatial instinct to urban survival, which allowed me to simply duck and dive; get this, sell that, for me, an alternative to the 9-5 that I simply wouldn't conform to - not now anyway. The alternative artist in me surfaced momentarily, and depending on your opinion, it allowed me to flourish favorably. I had acquired the skills as a competent forger and anything went; train tickets, books and cards, even money. Then, I found there was an incredible mark up in the world of drugs. It was never the class A stuff, more what I saw as the lesser of the evil in the drug world. Cannabis was in demand and an easy avenue to go down. What originally started small time, quickly moved into heavier, more profitable dealings. It went very quickly from a couple of eighths to a couple of kilos, and so on. In no time, what with the blues, speed, and my very entrepreneurial skills, my whole outlook to anyone with authority was to 'GO FUCK YOURSELF!'

Phenytoin 400 mg
Tegretol 200 mg

I remember the scene very well. It was amazing to be amongst what was very much an urban revolution, in the same as it was a breath of fresh air in the linear, everyday norm that was suffocating a new, younger more vibrant London. It was psychedelic T-shirts and old vintage 501's, Converse, nice weed, pot, hash, resin - thanks Howard AKA Mr. nice long hair, hippy hats and john Lennon glasses for College. Of course, I'm talking about Camden market. The epicenter of all that was good and new. Now as much as I try to justify my actions, I won't mix my words or lie. I had to earn, and the obvious way to me was to use my natural born talent of entrepreneurship, and what easier way than a trip into town and taking advantage of the high street stores and the high-end clothing outlets. They allowed me to re stock my wardrobe, but mostly to sell to the needy and the greedy. What was easily available, was nothing less than amazing discounted apparel for those with enough arsehole to gain the latest from the likes of Pierre Cardin, Ellesse, Farah, Adidas - you name it. Of course, now I'd stepped it up with the clothing, so I felt the same was needed with the drugs. Blues and speed made me feel a step higher in the cultural phenomena growing around me. The newly found income also allowed me more money for the pub or visits to football at west ham, all the while, these completely diverse environments and the fits were more frequent for both people trapped inside me.

Phenytoin 400 mg
Tegretol 600 mg

Well you can imagine how it ends up! April 10 1981, a few mates and me had met up in the plough pub in Cranham. I'd been on the piss all night, and since they were kicking off in Brixton, we decided we'd have some as well, what better way to spend a night out. Mates, alcohol, aggression and a row with the symbol of authority I'd come to hate. Within a couple of hours, it was rockin' and I was at the forefront of the riots. Old bill were getting pelted with cue balls, glasses and petrol bombs from the plough public house, the fire brigade had turned up and it was fucking mental. I felt like I was contributing into something revolutionary, amongst all the chaos, I believed I was investing in something new, but the fun was to end. Two plane clothes officers picked me up Sunday morning at 6 a.m. round my mate's house. I was arrested under the 1964 riot act. The outcome was detention centre, the 'short sharp shock', as they called it. Hollesley bay colony, near Norfolk for 8 weeks and my opening appearance to the judicial system. Bang up was from 9 p.m. to 6.30 a.m. you marched everywhere, 1 to a cell, and was constantly stitched up by the screws whenever they got the chance. An inmate grassed me up for adding sugar to my porridge, (which I'd saved from the top of a biscuit the night before) and to my surprise, was put on Governors Order and slung in the block that very same morning. A damp dingy cell was my home for three days and nights, with cardboard furniture, (to stop you damaging a screw) the low life officer produced a tin of tobacco in front of the governor, and a charge was read out. I was then asked," Is this your tin?" "Yes!" I replied. It was opened showing it full of sugar. I was charged (Stitch up) I was then given a further three days loss of remission and sent back to the block. I read 'My Story' by Ron Kray - fascinating character. Well life wasn't that bad, although to me I'd seen better!

    I returned to Cranham an infamous revolutionary, or so I thought, as I'd been highlighted in all the local papers to be some sort of rebel, much to my dear old mums' embarrassment. Nobody else was nicked, as I'd told the C.I.D, I hadn't known anybody else that night. I'd described them all as a lot older than me and we're wearing political activist black armbands, I had to laugh. An older chap took me in, giving me a place to stay. His name was Phil Dalby. I went to school with his brother Paul. Along with Martin Troy, Stevie Heron and Gary King who were also staying there, I was now in a better place. The lads were all West Ham and part of the bigger crew who made up the ICF.

    I'd been on a few away games to Manchester, Newcastle, Birmingham, you name it and with these boys, it always ended in a massive off. It was a bit daunting at first, and they put me through my initiation, including but not limited to hanging me over the balcony one day after giving them some lip, telling me to apologise or they would drop me...I did...and they still dropped me, just for a laugh. Then there was the time I came in late after breaking into a place, making off with a haul of boxes of burgers and sausages on a pal's Honda 90. I remember the wheels were stuffed full of paper, because it had a flat. I called it Phil's puncture repair kit. On my return home, they all told me the old bill had just raided the house looking for me, and I'd better leave.... So, I got my stuff, and apologised again for bringing it on top. Feeling my grief, they suggested I slept in the dog kennel for the night, just incase the old bill came back. "There's no way they'll look in there", they added. At the time it made sense, so a cold night was had with Max, a mean looking Doberman, drooling and salivating over me for nicking his bed. The morning came with me curled up in a ball, shivering and wishing I'd never nicked those fucking burgers. I then heard footsteps, 'this is it', I thought, I'm nicked. Then I heard Phil's voice quietly whispering, "Len, you'd better get going mate". I was just about to leave, when all of the lads fell about laughing making donkey sounds "EEEEAAWWWW!" Another initiation and lesson in 'don't shit on your own doorstep!'

All said and done, they were great blokes and took me in, Phil was like that. I'd had quite a few fits, and they were always supportive, even saved my life a few times after swallowing my tongue, there was one occasion I'd taken a chunk out of his hand! Phil told me "the next time I had a wobbler, he was going to chuck me in a bath of warm water and throw the washing in so as to clean them!", "that's if you've still got fingers", was my reply! Phil's education and lessons to anyone in his circle, was to always give as good as you got! He hated the bullies that existed and would always educate and prepare you for them.

Phenytoin 400 mg
Tegretol 800 mg

It wasn't long before I was starting my next stretch. 6 months to 2 years, after 3 months on remand in Chelmsford for a string of shops and warehouses and the odd motor. The whole process of being passed from one place to the next in the sweatbox, which carried you from court to court, was never fun, but then it isn't supposed to be! One notorious place I went through was the Old Bailey. Some of the biggest names in the British criminal fraternity had gone through there, and it was here, we picked up a few people who were given a ten, a couple of fives and a life sentence. The next step was Rochester for allocation, where it's decided what borstal you were assigned to and then your new home at the care of a new set of bullies in uniform. My family wrote, as did friends. A good mate called Andy Keates kept me updated regularly on what was happening on the outside. One thing I'd like to mention, I always appreciated letters from the outside. Anyone that's part of the human race and appreciates the pulse in his or her body, will tell you the value of a letter. You needed your letters and visits, especially as I'd been on the move for months. Any one that reads this and has friends or relatives on the inside, please invest in a letter to them. It means more than you know.

Lessons

23 and a half hours a day, banged up with meals in your cell, was my life now, and it was a total shit sandwich served daily. I'd witnessed some of the most game and intent violence dished out daily between inmates you could have imagined. If people got organized back then, the screws would've been fucked. It eventually dawned on me, a person's primate instinct has its place, and if you cage a person and abuse them like an animal they eventually will behave like one. One night, a con on the landing above me was crying, the other inmates taunted him with, "fuck off and do yourself" and "mummy's boy" and other uncaring remarks, it was really sad to hear. You can Guess what happened when it come to morning call. The inevitable was on the cards. As quick as the cell doors opened they were slammed shut. The poor bloke had killed himself! You had to understand, you were on your own in here, you had to get on with it and do it, the best way you could. The solitary done my head in, so I started to read a lot more and even managed to get my hands on a few more Krays books and many other infamous characters; Pretty boy Shaw, McVicar, Lenny McLean - The Guv'nor. I started to read a lot, anything I could get that was worth reading - true life, religion, Psychology, meditation, healing, therapies, anything to get my head out of this place and in the process, an all-round higher education

Phenytoin 400 mg
Tegretol 1000 mg

The meds were handed out every morning, they'd decided that my dose was to be increased and in liquid form. This didn't work very well, and I was fitting every other day. Eventually I was taken to the hospital wing for observation, where we got let out every 2 days for exercise with an even smaller yard than the main wing! It was a cross between One Flew Over the Cuckoos Nest and The Midnight Express, with half naked old men drugged to the eyeballs, inmates all staggering around the path mumbling and moaning and bumping into each other. That was until this 7ft skinny black, twenty something con shouted, "STOP!" We ground to a halt. "ONE WAY!" he then shouted and we followed suit. You had to find the funny side of life in here, or you cracked.

Jason Allday

The hospital visit had helped, and they allocated me to a semi open prison, for Young Prisoners at Huntington, near Reading. Which was to be my home for at least another year. Here, apart from the normal isolated prison fracas, everything was different. You had a work party, and trades you could enroll in. They had everything from bricklaying, plastering, painting and decorating, which I had a go at. Being the sharper than your average cat, and seeing an opportunity, I had a nice little sideline in portraiture for snout, which helped the weekly wage of around £2. Might as well make a few quid while under her majesty's care, eh! My parents were pleased and came to see me once a month, and we had also discussed on my release, I could go back and live with them. I was over the moon; I'd missed so much of family life. The letters telling about my sisters 21st birthday, Andrew going off to start his own business, Stephen's school results, I was missing a large part of their lives. They had clubbed in and bought me the Shalamar album for my birthday, which we could play in the recreation room. The African and Caribbean cons were all doing the Jeffrey Daniels body pop and moonwalk, they showed me all the moves, good times in a hellhole of a place. I left them the album, which I know they would've appreciated, and for those that remember me, I hope you played it until the screws went mad from hearing it so often.

Back home, I got into some work with a pal decorating and found it suited me, I'd come to realise I needed a job that suited my disability. I found this working on my own, finding strength in my independence, and accepting I had strength, once I'd identified my weakness. In the last few years, I'd had doors closed on my existence, as a result of my own actions. Well, now my actions will open those doors. I decided, I had the confidence and needed to chin up and soldier on. That edge, eventually gave me the confidence to being in the work place, and able to fit in again, all without a hoo-ha. It was perfect, or as best as it could be, and I soon got a job with Alfred McAlpines.

The rave scene had been going on a while now, and the hooligan element had died down - the lads had changed. "What's your team?", was now "What you on"? There was a new kid on the block. Ecstasy for the weekend; another mentalist movement! It made you think you were untouchable and part of a movement. Here I found a place, I was off the terraces to the clubbing with ya' mates - Oi, Oi Saveloy! That's the difference between E's and the rest of the world! Happiness isn't good enough for me! I demand euphoria! And it fucking was. Your senses exploded on the dance floor. Art played another part here, with the backdrops and through some mates, Rusty Rich, Tony T and a whole load of others we were part of it, organising, setting up, or going to as many raves as we could. It was around the time I met Leanne, a lovely girl and to be the mother of my daughter - later born Georgina Payne, my blood and my angel.

I was 27 and loved being a dad. She was such a pure and sweet thing, I absolutely loved her. I realised now, I had to give up some adopted behaviours, and as a few scenarios recently had ended up going wrong, and on a couple of occasions, I was getting seriously near to being nabbed again, I needed to reevaluate my standing. A rip off scumbag, no hoper, from another manor, had even recently stabbed me and retaliation was in order. It all started to get a bit hectic. The irony was, they called it the summer of fuckin' love! So, we moved out of the manor for a while to keep it real - the rollercoaster had gone on too long, I needed the teapot ride, so that's what we did, and it was the best move I ever made

Jason Allday

TOAST

I got back into my art again. Gina was about 2 or 3, I'd made her some toast, but I'd burnt it under the grill and found myself scraping off the black bits; nobody likes burnt toast and trying to get your kid to eat without imperfections, can be a challenge all in itself. So, I started playing with the idea of making the toast more appealing and interesting; I guessed smiley faces was the way to go. I noticed something in the process, although it sounds strange, I saw the cross over from shading and instantly, loaves started becoming my palette, placing the pieces of bread together and made a face burning, then scraping with a knife it started to come together. Leanne thought it was cool and my mate, Gary Sparks, came around and instantly liked it. So, we glued it to a board, and I had it kept at a flat I had over Rainham.

The fits were still as active as ever, and got more frequent. Having a child was brilliant, but having fits and a child was problematic. It was a bit of a waiting game once I'd had a fit, I could take her out and do stuff, but the waiting for the inevitable, increased my anxiety to the fit that hadn't even started, was also becoming as much of a fight as the fits themselves. This then started me to have ticks as well. The only way I can describe it, it's much like a type of jolt, I could have up to 50 a day. I tried to hide this new condition reasonably well, although it become interesting in a boozer once in a while, as I was prone to throw a pint at a sudden notice.

Lessons

It also made everything more debilitating, I was once again angry at life. All of my mates understood, and never took the piss, they all knew it was a burden for me, and they all helped, one way or another. It's then, you can identify with who is really there for you, your mates become more of your life and become everything you could wish for. I'd really tried to be strong, even with my earliest thoughts that I'd engaged in, and never forgot my years visiting Great Ormond Street, but it started to get to me. Well, of course, they upped the pills! I'd even contemplated the quick exit on my long walks with the dog over Havering park, but even though I was that down, and often depressed with everything, I knew your loved ones can't go through that, it wouldn't be fair to do that to them. I prayed a lot, and I don't care what you believe in, but when you are able to touch base with your inner self, mantra or whatever it is, sometimes some things just happen. For know I'll simply say, I was keeping it real and feeling the flow.

Phenytoin 400 mg
Tegretol 1200 mg

Leanne's Mum, Janet, had seen a program on the box about a surgery that could help with epilepsy. See what I'm saying, totally out of the blue. I was willing to try anything, so I pushed for a second opinion through my G.P. A few MRI and CAT scans later, and a visit to the National neurological hospital, yeah, again! So, Back to Queens Square in Holborn, to see a professor Duncan, head of neurology. He decided to put me on different pills for the tics, or jolts, and sent me off to the Chalfont centre for epilepsy observation. My first thought was they must be mad, as basically, they'd stop your pills and watch you fit, but what was I supposed to do? I owed it to my family and those that had always been there for me. The process was simple at first, the other patience and myself would play cards, and by the end of the game, three out of five of us would be on the deck, shouting, shaking or pissing them selves. I really warmed to them, there was a kind of security in it all, as there was no fear of being judged, sneered at or commented on - it was like living in a world of people that were all equal.

Phenytoin 400 mg
Tegretol 1000 mg

Lamotrogine 200 mg

More scans, and a couple of weeks past, my doctor gave me the news that it was a Glyomia - a type of tumor. Fuck, was my first thought! What the fuck now, what didn't I have wrong with me? It turned out it was non-malignant, (not cancerous) which was a relief, but this was the reason for the fits. It was a type of growth, and it had been sitting there, giving out its own electricity, sparking off when it felt like it, and had been growing steadily from birth. The news doesn't get any better, as I'm then being told, there's 6 months wait to see a surgeon.

Mr Harkness, at the National, advised me after looking at the results, there was a strong possibility of offering me an operation. Finally, something I can say was good news. I went there with my mate Charley Mason, and after the appointment, we went and had a beer in Holborn. I was over the moon, and, if I'm being honest, I cried like a baby, as at long last, this horrible affliction was to leave me forever.

Surgery was available in July of 1999, Steve Trotter, a great man, who with his own disabilities, had supported me through the years. He took me up there a couple of days before Gina's birthday, she was only 7. I remember I had gone out and bought her a bike just before, and gave it to her as a treat, she didn't understand what it was all about. The day arrived, and I decided to have a very long prayer to the man above. I had the start of several brain surgeries, to partially remove what had been growing in the parietal lobe. I can remember coming back to the ward, my right side was numb, and they had given me a smaller chance of a complete seizure free life. After the first op, they said there was a 1 in 3 odds of success, but I still wanted the 2nd op. I wanted to fight this, I wanted to know I'd tried and not wonder the rest of my life how it might have turned out. The numbness eventually subsided to only my right foot. I thought I'll live with that, and overall, a fucking miracle! To be totally honest, in many ways, it redesigned my whole life, to say I owe these people, is an understatement.

After Gary moved to Wales, I went down there, and had another go at some more 'Toast art'. This was around 2002, and the rave scene was getting busier. I was also organising backdrops and themed nights and with our own 'Avit do's work coming in on a regular basis, the lads, Richard Milton and Tony T, all decided an Arty break was in order. Well the outcome was awesome, 'F9 Generic Disorder', a self portrait (got the code off my constantly crashing gas boiler) and the 'Madonna purity', something we're all born with, got a coating of resin, as Gary had been working with resins and carbon fibers. It essentially acted as a sealant. After I'd finished, I took the train home from Wales with the toast in a plastic D.J Album box, and set them out. Later, I mounted them with glue. Wales was a great place to go and chill, and over the years my best art has come out of there. It was weird, but in the mountains and fresh air, away from the 'London scene', everything was much clearer - It had a natural energy I could feed from, and so much space.

Once home, I got to framing the Pieces, and a friend suggested I send the images to the art and illustration magazine. Would you believe it, they actually showed it in the next issue. Shortly after, a meeting with some big wigs on Fleet Street materialised, and another with Saatchi, who were amazed, but I had only 2 pictures to show for my Toast artwork exhibition. It had never been seen, remember, this style was totally unique and had never been done before. What were my thoughts? No words can encapsulate that feeling! I was advised to put one in a Dorking Art Gallery with a price of £1200. F9 went to a charity Auction at Bonham's, for the National hospital development foundation and sold for £1400. I took Gina along, who was now 11. It was an emotional night for me to be in such a Grand Place, with my Toast Art, sipping champs and for such a worthy cause. I felt I had given something back to the foundation, which had helped me so much. I couldn't put into words my appreciation or gratitude, so for me, this was one way I could simply say, thank you. I received two further commissions for £1500 each, and an offer from an agent called Patrick Davies.

Patrick came down to south Hornchurch, and liked what he'd seen, but wanted a cleaner look and a better sealant Finnish. He then told me to go off and create some pieces for the London Art Fair, and in the meantime, he would talk to his framer, to come up with a solution, which turned out very successful. Now I encase all toast work in a polymer resin, the framing still stays the same. I found tremendous opposition, whilst acquiring studio space, as many a well-healed studio manager remarked, on how many artists are financially helped by their parents, and have been through university but don't have an agent and were unable to understand where I'd come from. This made me recall my knowledge of the impressionist, who struggled to compete with the hierarchy, for the Salon de Paris. The rent was so high, but affordable, from my opportunity to work in Alencon, in France for a couple of months where I was renovating a chateau I stayed in. It was an amazing old stable with an upper balcony. You see, most people can't actually see the image, when you're working on it. Yeah, I know, pretty weird, and I can only assume from my short-sighted ability to see at different levels of optical vision, and having an over active imagination, I was able to work with this media, and master its technique at close proximity. Everyone else was forced to view it from the balcony.

I worked on the Rokoby Venus, but with a twist. She held a mirror, (on the original there was a face) on mine, there was the tree of life and on her behind, was a tattoo of a serpent. I called it 'Temptation', my view on the world of Drugs and urban decay. Why do we go there? I believe it's mans natural behaviour, to be tempted by the 'inner demons'. I did a retake on the Madonna, and another with two fish, I called it '5 loafs', and a Picasso influence type piece, called 'Desire'.

The London Art Fair was on a Wednesday night, buyers and artist were present and I 'smashed it'! They sold every piece for five grand! My mate Tony came with me that night, and we got blathered on the free beer. While Patrick introduced me to clients and prospective buyers, I waffled my way through the process; the sealing and framing and the obvious 'why toast?' speech. Some were amused, some in awe of this exciting new media, and I enjoyed it, even more knowing I wasn't about to have a fit and smash something out of the way, damage or smash myself up. I'd had a couple of minor seizures since the operation, but mostly controlled, and it meant for the first time, I could stand there feeling important, proud, confident and without a care in the world. Something I hadn't experienced in a very, very long time.

The Art fair was a complete success, and Patrick took pieces off to fairs around the world, and had many an interest. I had magazine articles appearing everywhere, and so decided to make a website. It was good for worldwide media attention and commissions, and I was now spending days and nights perfecting this new media, and getting the work out for the clients.

A chance meeting with a band called Motty's Sheapskin, who had bought out a cover of the 'hurry up Harry' song, originally done by Sham 69, lead to me being a proud contributor to an event, hosted by Gary Bushel. Gary was setting up a 'battle of the bands' event, so as to auction off donated work, for the raising of enough money to have a Benny Hill statue commissioned. The event was held at the Purfleet Tavern, with a host of quality lads, including The Cockney Rejects. It was Jesus John, Andre Evens and Pat Geary who originally suggested I make a Benny Hill on toast, so we could Auction it at the event. Gary loved it, and the artist 'Right Said Fred', was the highest bidder. It was covered in The Sun, and most of the tabloids worldwide. The website was Buzzing, and I'd been asked to do some interviews on the radio including BBC Essex, and burn some toast in the interval. My local papers and then the BBC picked it up, and with all this attention, asked me to do an interview and documentary for the Inside Out program. Then David Leigh, the Art Critic for the Times, came around to the studio. I was interviewed and filmed creating a piece called 'Why Wait for Heaven', it was an interesting opportunity for me. I thought if they were to show it on the box, it had to be controversial, thought Provoking, or at least I had a crack at using the media for an interesting message.

Why Wait for Heaven?

'Why wait for heaven', in toast, was a naked woman nailed to a tree, signifying her crucifixion. Some art has a different meaning, or interpretation, although this particular piece has a very definite meaning for me, and for religion as a whole. You're given a trade by religion, eternal life. Where and what does it look like? It's probably that sandy golden shore. Beautiful sunshine? Yep, that will do me! If you ask yourself if you believed in heaven, what's your vision? Probably is somewhere you cherished, maybe cornfields, Wales? But what if it's not there, what if it never was, what if the most beautiful place you ever going to, lived, breathed, existed is actually here! So why don't we put these prehistoric dated scriptures to one side!

Jason Allday

Did you know, 95% of the world believes in something, FACT! So, my thought, is let's accept a new cosmic, holistic approach to humanity, and agree religion is outdated and realise, that this here today, is our heaven, and we only have one heaven and here It is. So, I have to ask, why the fuck are we crucifying mother earth?

'A revolution with toast'

Keppra 500
Lamotrogine 200

We followed it up with a solo exhibition at the Air Gallery in Piccadilly, All very exciting. A few friends and family were invited, I felt very important, and if I'm honest, I thought I'd cracked it, but humbly, you realise you've only just stepped onto the bottom rung. I'd entered another piece into the Royal Academy, around that time Ian Jury, the Lord of Upminster. I'd started to do this as a print through my local framers, a 1/10 - another spin off.

I was then asked by Marmite through an email, to help with a campaign for 'love it or hate it'. They were all jumping on the 'Toast Gig', by then my agent put me off, saying it wasn't going to be any help for my 'art career', and I agreed (he was the boss, only not an honourable one!) only to find as the documentary came out, at the very same gallery, was the very same thing, all be it a very second rate go at my 'Art with Toast' but rather than burnt with a blow torch and with gently scrapping, it was Marmite! I'd been sold out. Fair play to Marmite. But Patrick's underhandedness had riled me, and his Mrs. worked in PR. You see, the PR and advertising held more dough (small joke). I was pissed off, and went around to Patrick's and took back anything he still had and 'politely' wished him good day. I was told by my mum to get into bakers. It made sense and as mum added "you can promote each other". I got Pat to put it on the website, he'd helped me loads over the years. He had a lot going on himself, he had a young family and a group going, called the Chummyfuds, but it didn't stop him from coming up trumps yet again, top man! At the same time, for a while anyway, I had ago in the film industry as a set artist. Rupert Alan gave me a job for a day on a production called Mile High, at Three

Mills studio, Bow. My first job was to make a ten by five-meter floor of MDF look-like. It was to made to look like old warehouse floorboards, more forgery I thought. After a day, I cracked it, and I stayed there for about 3 months. Then I landed job with Paul Burns, the Art Director at Vertigo films, who'd been part of the 'football factory' and 'all gone Pete Tong'. We worked on Namastey, London, dream team - I loved it and really appreciated these chaps giving me a break. They knew I had a bit of a short fuse for piss takers, and Rupes had seen me knock out a two-bob bouncer in his local club on the front in Wales, and it was acknowledged, I was a bit of a live wire, truth is, I'd had the upmost respect for them all, and I think they eventually looked at me like a breath of fresh air. I took Gina down to the set of Bad Girls, a massive prison in a warehouse. It was so lifelike, reminding me of the past, and how things had changed. I worked with Sami Khan on a load of films, even as art director on Take me Back with Jonty Kenton. I envied and admired these guys in some way, it felt I'd been denied this type of lifestyle in my choices of the path I'd taken, or the cards your dealt, but that's life I suppose. It's how you play your hand that counts. 'Keeping it real', was Sami 's advice.

The website was paying off well, I'd had a few enquires with company's asking if I could do stuff with ice cream, chips, oil, you name it. Finally, I got a bite, mum was right. I got an email from a P.R company, working with Warburtons on, with a view, to do Simon Cowell, Louis Walsh, Danny Minogue and Cheryl Cole on Toast for 8k. As I was doing this, up come another job for pumpkin carvings, for a fright night event at £500 each, they wanted 10! Four appeared on the X factor of the judges, 1 of Alan Carr, for the loose women show, and the other five were off to Alton Towers. It gave me the cash to invest in my own exhibition, not that I wasn't happy with work in general, and I loved the set work. I felt I'd slipped away from 'real art'. I'd done a lovely piece called 'Taste That', to the local constabulary titled 'say it in toast not petrol'. It was a masked man throwing a toaster. Another piece called 'Bread Line', a type of organic self-producing abstract piece, and my interpretation of a slow deterioration of long-term substance abuse. I was still feeling the need to unwrap the inner cortex, due to an earlier trauma, or just to simply explore different paths, and taunt my, or others own believes, if not to produce something more worthy than Simon Cowell, who in my mind has catapulted the music industry, into a molten mush of mess. There was a lot of exploratory work I knew I had in me, and I still thought I needed to express myself.

I had a particularly strange experience in my late 20's, with the onset of a seizure, I had gone to the Jobbers rest in Cranham, near by, was a cow field, and rather than smashing the surrounding tables and glasses whilst convulsing, I decided it'd be better to take a relaxing walk, slow my breathing, which I'd learnt over the years would calm the anxiety, and sit quietly on soft grass. My head had been struggling for years with the whole religion thing, (I suppose I had this 'Why Me?', issue going on) now the thoughts started filling my head, starting with 'what's the meaning of it all?', and 'why are we here.com?'. I suddenly came to a clump of grass on one side of the field, I sat there breathing slowly and turned to my right and there was a candle and an egg, which I naturally thought was very strange. I walked away bemused by my vision and the penny just dropped! Sorry, but you'll have to work that out yourself, I haven't enough space here, but I will say, what if religion is a conflict of a very nice upstart, or two from different centuries and parts of the world? Who knew we just had to love each and every fellow man, share, care and appreciate the world where we all live and all and everything is one. What if we are all in a big hamster wheel, what if we aren't? Maybe I just think too much, but I suppose that's what artists do! I knew I had to produce my own Exhibition, examine these areas of belief, evolve and experiment.

I was now off to Cyprus to work, much like Wales, it was a place to chill. Over the next few months, the time away allowed me to produce an amount worthy of an exhibition. My old pal Phil was out there, and I was always happy to see him. He was part of my still being here and had always been there for me since the old days. They had put me up on a farm, with my own studio, it was a daunting challenge to say the least, but I put my head down and cracked on. It was here for the first time in a long while, I could just focus and home my skills, reinvent, establish and create a worthy art collection. I sent the whole lot back on Cyprus Airways for about 300 euros, telling them it was just a few old pictures. It was scanned and delivered to Heathrow the following day without a scratch. A few more months in Wales, where I'd created the Amy Winehouse piece, which has always been a favourite of mine. On my return, some friends put me in

Lessons

touch with Lawrence Watson, Noel Gallagher's photographer. Noel personally endorsed a picture that he gave Lawrence, which was a good piece for the press to pick up on, and free advertising for the big day. What with a picture of Amy Winehouse, and Howard Marks, who attended on the night, it was good publicity. I had the artwork valued by an independent buyer within the art-world, and in all, documented, it was worth over £180,000; around 5K to 15k each - WOW! With an installation, which I produced in a warehouse in Hainault, we were ready to rock. I say 'We', as there were many individuals on the pay roll. Through Brixton Paul, I'd acquired a PR firm, from Manchester, who had rented me a warehouse, and I'd used this for making another life size replica of the Coronation streets Rovers return pub in Bread for another of Warburtons Advertising campaigns; another nice little earner of 14k!

Arthur, who was the owner, had a scrapyard, just down the road, was a complete gentleman of the 'old school', and had done his fare share back in the day. His brother, Jimmy, was part of the infamous Quality Street Gang, who were a very well-known outfit in Manchester, did a lovely job, with some organising. I allowed them some branding here and there, which was only fair. Paul sourced an exhibition showroom in Shoreditch, called the Maverick - not cheep at 5K a week from Angelo, who was a cool Italian/German. He'd had regular shows, and knew the market, and offered to introduce some buyers to the opening night. So, in my mind, a good call and London was buzzing at the time with emerging new artists. Reuters got in touch, and requested an interview, which went worldwide, Blimey! They covered the story on ABC news in the states, and the night was a huge success, with a completely packed House, heaving with journalists, magazine publishers and tabloids. Grimey from Radio 1 along with family, friends and a few celebs', all finished off at McQueens as an after-party. All well received and with opening nights sales, I couldn't have been more chuffed.

This exhibition marked a night in my life, brought about a childhood ambition, passion and personal achievement. A medium, such as burnt bread, crossed over from being a tabloid novelty, and became a personal voice and canvas, to a planet, where action needs reflection, was my humbling approach to my second go at a Solo exhibition. 'Food for thought', a piece on the night of a starving child made with bread. Toast, a metaphor for the basic human need to eat and survive, also exist as a canvass, on which to explore the spirituality that influences and effects our every day lives. Yeah, you could say I made a few statements! "The thing about art, is not what the medium is, but what the picture is about, and if you can really get the attention and have the voice, what would you say?", was my quote on the radio the next day. My mum was chuffed, when I showed her the video of the night on the Website, she told all of her friends. I had realised over the years, she truly had my best interest at heart all along, as many people did. Dad passed away years ago, as has mum. They were both smashing parents, angels in my eyes.

There have still been ups and downs, 2 steps forward, 3 steps back, not ten as it used to be. I'd had a chunk of money with regards to art sales go walkies through a few odious characters, which eventually always gets dealt with, and Karma played its card in the end. But after such a massive event there's always follow up work, with commissions, radio, and magazine articles. You see, when you have an article written by Reuters, they distribute worldwide, so I started getting emails from Africa to Hong Kong. The same exposure also lead me to being involved with the Ray Lowry Foundation exhibition. This exhibition provides funding to aspiring art students. Others contributed included artists such as The Clash, Pennie Smith and Harry Hill among other performers and writers. We all donated new works that would be auctioned In Tokyo. This was important to me, giving back to something I valued, and was proud to be involved in. There was another project that I considered very worthy and an honour to be part of, this time in north Cyprus for the Children's Cancer Hospital in Lefkosia, where I was asked to do a picture made out of pitta bread, by Mustafa Hurses. I even got to meet the President, an amazing experience; he gave me a present and congratulated me for coming, and being part of their campaign. The whole procedure was shown live on Turkish TV. The Picture sold to a banker and raised 7k towards this event, and for me, another chance to help out and give to someone more deserving. Warburtons got in touch again, but by this time, my whole family had just moved over to Cyprus. We had to fly back, and create a London skyline installation in 2013, which had a load of exposure. There have been many interesting evolvements, Auctions, commissions and a call from Alex

Lessons

Barendregt, an interesting fella, who runs a festival each year in Austria called the World Body Painting Festival. Jesus John and me drove out there with 40 loaves, aptly named 'Jesus and the 40 Loaves Tour'. Orla Deone was singing and I had pre-decided to do her portrait on stage, in front of a 10,000 strong 'not bad for an epileptic from Cranham' I thought.

I'm always experimenting with new media I've used paint Chipping's to create some other styles. 'Nymthalidae', 'Astral Angel', and 'Kevira', which I've sold as prints. I'm often asked to paint portraiture in oils, which is something I enjoy doing. The more hours I spend, I realise, you could spend a lifetime mastering these technics. I've started to developing 'an ashes to art', which I'm in the process of experimenting on, the journey is still not over, art wise, there's been a lot of interest in prints Commissions and new projects

I had a trip down to Wales last year with my wife, and we were in a pub in Aberystwyth, and we got chatting to a cousin of Charles Bronson. Straight away, I remembered my original exhibition, and wondered if he thought Charlie would be interested? So, after saying hello to his mum Ira, I wrote to Charlie, and would you believe it, he replied! He told me he now likes to be called Charles Salvador, as a mark of respect to one of his favourite artist Salvador Dali. Charles Bronson earned the title 'Britain's most violent Inmate', or so they say, and has spent 40 years behind bars - most of them in solitary. I've the utmost respect for him, (and so do many) for everything I've mentioned and been through myself, seems immaterial to this man's unlawful incarceration. He's never had an easy day inside, he never murdered anyone!

Charlie's picture.

There are things in the making, and it's all a process, but let me leave you with this - Maybe the journey isn't so much about becoming anything. Maybe it's about unbecoming everything, that isn't really you, so you can be who you were meant to be in the first place.

Live long, don't let a rough start in life dictate what you want to be, and simply become what you can be.

Jason Allday

A casual state of mind

In industry, appropriate dress is one of the most common associations made to professionalism, in the world of business it's an essential doctrine - all be it superficially, as your appearance can inspire a level of confidence and attitude, the very same appearance allows the bank clerk or manager to attain a level of respect from those within the financial community, it sets a bench mark and clothes makes the man! In society a sense of who you are, is gained by the way you dress. Fundamentally your presentation says who you are. It's Part of the mechanics - a cog in the wheel. Being smart and your efforts in your cotton 'n threads is like putting meat on the bone. For the early working class, it allowed them to get the upper hand on the socially superior middle class.

Each and every generation boasts an ideology and a trend, teddy boys, mods, skinheads, all carried a way about them, each claiming to promote a philosophy superior to its predecessor, but none has outlasted or made an impression more than the casual movement. It was an aggressive sub culture that in many cases demanded more from the wearer than the observer - it wasn't a part time gig for some, you always had to stay ahead, and for the chap in the equation, would make themselves the biggest critique and judge. Casual wear extended from the terraces to the world beyond. It allowed you to carry your swagger after the row and in turn it become your own identity. No one could argue, being dapper or smart enabled you to be a betterment to society, as your personal individualism and identity could be gained from this movement.

There were even some lads that'd keep certain outlets/ boutiques 'quiet' in an attempt to stay ahead and gain new and exclusive gear. A couple of lads would later testify that as much as they looked forward to a tear - up with a visiting firm, on the sly they'd see what they were wearing. Some Individuals would raise the bar - out doing each other in many cases with trips to mainland Europe to get unheard or scene numbers. Like most lads, dropping a few hundred on a few new outfits, whether it be Sergio Tacchini, Fila or Stone Island, it instilled a level of confidence. A college degree was for some an investment, others saw a week's wages on a pair of trainers and jacket as equally important.

By all standards, being a football casual bettered who you were. The working class created a new society and until mainstream cottoned on it was an undetected and unknown youth culture. Casual clothing was an integral part of football and the youth movement, and as time would prove, it intertwined with football hooligan history. The power and gain in confidence can be attributed to something you were in control of.

Something that by your own involvement allowed you to rise above the norm. It instilled as much dedication as discipline, and as much politics, music and drugs were part of the parcel, the dresser typically needed only a few things to truly promote how he stood and that was his attitude, a few quid and a platform we all called football casuals.

Jason Allday

Rob Silvester

"There has to be compatibility or a divided house will fall"- U.S political address

I was born in Finchley, north London, on the 12th of September in 1964. So, there's no questions what my mum and dad were up to on Christmas Eve 1963! Mum was an east end girl, born in 1930's Shoreditch, and my dad was born in 1927 in Leytonstone, it's funny to think that my birth certificate reads that my dad was a detective sargeant (more about him later). Shortly after my arrival, we all moved to Orpington in Kent, but by 1970, mum and dad divorced, so both mum and me ended up moving to Portsmouth, family was as much of my family's survival and success and I'm glad they were there for us. The move to Portsmouth was an obvious choice for mum, because my mum's siblings had emigrated to the USA, and her mum, my nan, wouldn't fly and would only get the boat back across whenever she would return home. Some time later, she moved back home to the UK. Being only 6, the change of scenery and move was an easy transition and being a young boy, this to me was nothing more than a new adventure. It certainly had its advantages, as now I was only a bus ride from the beach. Here I also sort of come of age at Stamshaw school as the new kid. I think adjusting was successful being I had good family and what youngster doesn't like the thought of the beach in the summer?

My dad used to come down and take us back to Orpington every other weekend, and at the time, dad being an avid Spurs fan, we would often go and watch them with him, also thrown in as a bonus, he'd use his MET/ police contacts. This perk allowed dad to conveniently park in Tottenham magistrates car park, even on a Saturday, this proved to be advantages as now we was parked much closer to the ground. Thinking back, with my dad being old bill, this should've been a big conflict with me and my social involvement at football, but I guess I identified with the fact he was my dad first, and the rest was to accepted as secondary. As the years went by, and even up to the age of 13/14, I was still getting picked up by my dad, but by now he'd moved to Sevenoaks, it was also around this time that he was sharing stories of him in world war 2, and how he single handedly defeated the Germans, but the main story was how he had risen to a D.I in the flying squad, only to be busted down to station sergeant in the early '70s, when major corruption charges were bought against many high ranking flying squad officers. I'd often wondered where all the free cup final tickets came from, and how I always managed to have a cup final program. I honestly thought it was because the A.B.A finals were usually held the night before the cup final, at the old Wembley arena. So, makes you think, that having a tattoo doesn't necessarily make you a criminal, but wearing a tie doesn't make you honest.

I eased my way into young adulthood and found I was slowly getting into trouble at school, all the makings of a London scrapper, simply further south, well, it's like they say, 'you can take the boy out of London, but never London out of the boy'. One summer holiday I was up at dad's place and he asked me, "is there anything you want to do?" I had already been to a few Portsmouth home games and read they were away to Peterborough for their first game of the season, this was probably around 1976. For me it was a no brainier and a simple question of, "when can we leave?" and was music to my ears, when he said, "yeah, lets go, it's only a couple of hours away". So off we went in a big old rover 3500. I can remember being gutted because I didn't have a scarf to show my colours, a thought I've had, was this the start of my wanting to identify with a football 'look'? Anyway, about half way through the first half it started going off in the away end. The Pompey lot were giving it to the old bill and my old man commented, "look there's football agro!" I said "yeah I see it all the time at Fratton park". I had too, as in that first season I started going, Pompey always came out on top at home. I'd heard all the stories while hanging about outside the pubs where we lived.

Things were basically the same for the next couple of seasons, I went to loads of home games, then in 1978 my mum said she would pay for me and a few mates to go to the pictures. I ended up going to Aldershot away. On the train with a mate, I was amazed at seeing grown men pissed, trying to have it with old bill, stewards and a few Aldershot that were brave enough to see what Pompey were all about. Portsmouth always had a good away following, something that a few of us got involved with a few years later. The one thing I gained from this, was the friendship and security that typically would've been gained from a dad at home, was compensated by some of the most loyal people I've ever had around me. Like minded, maybe, but having someone that'll be there in time of need, is something I'll always give credit to.

It was around my school years that we started going to home games, this was around '75/ '76 and going up the Fratton end (Pompey's home end) getting involved with singing and seeing the odd scuffle in the ground at the away end, but we were straight home after the games, unaware that the home end used to empty pretty quick and run up to the Milton end to see if there were any takers for them. We used to hear about Pompey's firm through some of the older boys from our area, and how the famous battles Pompey had been involved in from the original skins at Blackpool in the late '60s and '70s, and the taking of Cardiff's end in '73, and of course the regular taking of Southampton's ground. Back then, the nearest I had come to football violence, was witnessing a saint's fan getting chased down Fratton Rd on our way home and getting a good kicking right in front of us. Seemed strange, seeing these older boys with flares and platform shoes all toeing him in, we were never in any danger or chance of trouble being that close to the incident, simply because we were Pompey, only youngsters being about 13, and the simple fact we were on foot, we couldn't have been anywhere else.

Lessons

Fashion at the time was slowly changing with the punk explosion, but there was more of a noticeable change in appearance with the football crowd. When I went to football or down the town center, I'd see geezers and birds with dyed hair and mad clothes. By the time I had reached 15, I had become a regular at football, but maintained a simple routine of more home games and the occasional away game, if it wasn't too far away. It was at this time that the 2-tone fashion kicked in, prompting a return of the skinheads to the terraces. I was still at school, but I decided I'd make an effort and got a no.1 haircut, Harrington jacket, black school trousers and cherry red doc martens. My commitment to the terrace culture had truly begun.

The football terrace scene at Fratton park was speeding up too, as aggro' was everywhere and wasn't limited to first hand experience, it was on the tv, national newspapers, the radio news, and in addition, the riots had started in Brixton along with C.N.D demos, National front marches, Grundig, strikes, it seemed all the headlines were about violence. I was getting older and involved with mates a few years senior to my own age, and I'd just left school, so it's without question, I was getting more aware of the cultural going ons. So, there was typically a discussion on the violence amongst us, plus as we were now going in pubs we would mix with all sorts of people from the city. The main topics were football clobber, music and birds. No doubt, the same as every other group of like-minded people up and down the country, I guess it's what some would call a social trend. We started drinking near to the main train station on home games, waiting for any news of other firms turning up, purely to see if they 'wanted it' and have a look how they were dressed! The top boys in the towns of the 1983 through 1985 seasons, were some of the best dressed firms in the lower leagues at the time, and only being 75 miles from London, it wasn't hard to keep up with the casual look. See, the thing that was easily missed or not known back then by main stream media; we were trouble by interpretation, but by some measure, there was a competition between as many of us, as other firms at bettering ourselves and raising our standards by our presentation and dress code; the high street shops that condemned us 'hooligans' certainly didn't waste anytime in capitalising on our ideas.

Over the years there were plenty of encounters with Millwall. It was a given, that if we were traveling through London, typically at Waterloo station, we'd bump into them. It become kind of a ritual and expected, that their firm would be up for it, and I always believed at any opportunity given, their main firm would be waiting for us. We always wore trainers at football, but I'd noticed Millwall's older lot always seemed to have a nice pair of shoes on, they looked menacing in my eyes, they made an effort on two fronts; turning up and dressed for the part. We played Millwall a few times in the early '80s and had equally as many battles with them, and even getting to know a few of them a few years later. One of our close mates, that regularly made trips to London for clothes, had a few England games under his belt, home and away, told us to go shopping in London and gave us a few areas to head to and what to look for. This was at the time of what could be classed as the more 'dressier' casual gear with Gabbicci, Lyle and Scott and if you made the effort, you could get a nice lambs wool diamond jumper in a gentleman's shop near east street market off the old Kent road. Excuse the pun, but the whole casual scene 'fitted' me nicely, I think the complexities of adult life weren't something I understood as a young boy, and I obviously related more to the disciplines of a terrace casual (and of course the irony) than the son of a police officer.

1986 onwards was mad, as people were now getting jailed for football disorders, as well as other things. You had stories being broadcast about England fans causing chaos, the Scottish clubs misbehaving, the miners strike, every time you put the tv on there was aggro, nothing had really changed except the price of a pair of trainers and the style of terrace wear. We still went to football and the clothes were still changing from sports gear in '84 to brighter colours of Benetton and naf-naf, as well as coloured Lois cords or drab Farah golf slacks. A new direction or a bit of fine tuning with the casual scene, had started to take place, as now lads started to wear trainers with trousers and what also started to be common place, was polo shirts with tracksuit bottoms. This was the mid '80's; boys turning up at games in blazers, Aquascutum shirts and Burberry golf jackets was becoming regular too. Maybe too expensive to get ruined in a row, but that didn't matter, that was the clobber and the scene, and people had it on at football, I guess you could say 'if you can't afford to replace it, don't wear it!' A Benetton shop opened up in south-sea, but it didn't last that long,

Lessons

Winchester was next! Turning up at football for some firms was a bit hit and miss after that, but with Portsmouth's 6.57 firm, a good mob was guaranteed at home and away, time proved (and also by the papers reports) that there had been aggro' caused by Portsmouth's 6.57 crew all over the country for a good few years, and already were building on a strong reputation for turning up; casually dressed and game for a row.

There had been a lot of arrests connected to the 6.57 crew due to their antics, from starting race riots, to outbreaks of serious disorder at Waterloo station with our old friends Millwall, that consistent behavior started to gain unwanted mainstream attention, and in turn spurned serious repercussions from the prime minister, that lead to jail for football hooligans in her era. Here's some conveniently forgotten history, and oh, the irony, the 6.57 crew even had a candidate for the elections, that caused major upset for a local councilor, apart from the re-count ordered by the 6.57, the general behavior ended up with a few ejections from the guildhall.

Things were getting more and more organised, not only with Pompey, but it seemed every team in the leagues now had a "firm". Whether it was 20-30 or 200-300, we were turning teams over, but funnily enough coming unstuck at places we never even knew had a following, not alone a firm. Lincoln was one example, when we turned up there expecting a walk in the park and they came at us from all angles, even throwing darts at us in the ground! We were untouchable at home, but after the events in the Heysel stadium, the whole football hooligan game changed. Instead of getting £100 fines, you were now going to prison, and without question, we had our fair share of bird handed out. We were pulling mobs of 150 plus for home games, and apart from Birmingham at home one year, we more than defended Portsmouth. The local police were blaming every bit of aggro' in the town on the 6.57 crew, some justified some not, but it didn't stop the local magistrates dishing out some severe penalties! There were a lot of rumors about dawn raids, so panic set in, and people were hiding scrapbooks, photos and more than likely a few tools. Here also another valuable lesson, no one I associated with at football ever grassed! If you're in, you're in, if you got your collar felt, you took it on the chin! It sickens me to think, why would anyone turn on the very people that were there for you! What does that say about a person, who folds under pressure; they themselves were a part of? Who you are as a lad, is more than likely who you'll be as an adult! A couple of raids did happen, but typically focused on alleged disorders at single games and not over a series or multiple games. We kept hearing as well, that the court hearings involving teams cases, had been (thankfully) collapsing, and as a result, a lot of compensation was being paid out by various police forces up and down the country (who would of thought some would earn from their terrace antics!) The agro' and clobber was still all the rage, and for most was the sole concentration. Going into the 2nd half of the '80's, and this was easily seen, a lot of the boys had been going to England away games, with Pompey flags being seen flying at every world cup since Spain '82; the England team has always been well supported by Pompey. No question, patriotism and football was in our veins.

Pompey were still causing havoc up and down the country, but like most things, change was just around the corner, time and lifestyle choices started to dictate who'd go to a game for a tear up. On some cases, less of the original 6.57 crew were now turning up for regular games, and typically only favouring a chance against our arch old enemy.

Millwall. For some, this was thought as the end of a good thing, then when '87 rolled in, bang! Another change and development occurred, when a few of the boys watched Pink Floyd in the old Wembley stadium and got talking to some local lads, who recommended to try an 'acid house gig'. It was there that it was suggested, the next time they were up that way, to give a few named venues a visit. The next thing you know, there were mobs of Pompey all over London, following this new social trend simply known as 'raves'. The rest was just mind boggling, with hardened terrace hooligans frequenting places, with the old enemy, all loved up laughing about the aggro' and rivalries, with conversations on who done who, and sharing the same floor space that not long before, would've been fought over. The only thing that slowed football violence for a while was ecstasy; who'd thought that a little white pill and music pumping, would change the opinions and actions of some proper violent people. Margret Thatcher could've saved a fortune of taxpayer's money, instead of the over policing of football grounds and stiffer sentences, she could've cashed in on the deal with the big warehouses and a very lucrative drug industry. The other very noticeable change, was the one discipline I related to, and that was the clobber. It had now changed into a retro hippy look; a less agreeable and less smart look. Chic and dapper was now baggy and scruffy. So, we'd gone through an un welcomed change with the face of football and the followers; a very 'casual' or 'looking the bollocks' when turning up for weddings, racing or a court appearance to a grunge, baggy look and the intermixing with other known hooligans. For a lot of us, our opinion was it had run its course, a lot of the 6.57 simply didn't agree with the intermixing with other firms and their known faces. A lot of us didn't want to hear stories of "I was on a couple with so and so at the weekend".

It goes without saying, that somewhere, they were still the boys, still turning up and making a show and still getting the 6.57 somewhere on a Saturday morning. Some of the boys were just getting home and still joined the ranks, it didn't really divide anyone, but generally it wasn't accepted, but life went on. The drums always beat when a firm was needed, my friends have remained as loyal as they day we caught the first train out of Portsmouth, and as much as the isolation and issues a divorce can promote with a young lad, being a football casual or hooligan, instilled a level of discipline, that if I'm honest, I don't think I'd found anywhere else, it was something that built confidence in a lot of lads across the country, taught you who you was and it was something that I related to. It's also this experience and confidence I've carried my whole adult life and would say to a degree, it's attributed to my current success in life.

Jason Allday

Bullying is universal

The irony, in what we stand for, and in many cases oppose, can be in itself, an irony! There's not been a time in a single person's life, that from even the most mildest of opinions, that a sane minded person will stand by or justify, by act of thought or action, reinforce or condone one of the most common traits seen throughout not only the animal world, but also in modern day society - bullying!

Throughout our lives, with the inherent dangers and pitfalls of inner-city life, we are, if not conditioned but accepting to the many types of oppressive acts of human behavior. One of the ugliest traits seen within the every day workings of our lives, is a less fortunate or weaker person becoming a target of a stronger, bigger or simply less civilized person's actions. One of the first thoughts or actions is to fix the situation and act on the victim's behalf; but then isn't the repercussion it self an act of bullying? Some could argue that here you're not only acting as a stronger, bigger and less civilised person (as laws were enacted to prevent miss placed acts of street justice), but it could also be argued that you yourself are acting in an equally bullying way.

So, when and where do you draw the line with regard to stepping in? For many, there's a simple method or test in when and where they should act. Your morals and integrity are yours and yours alone. No one person should be allowed to manage or take those two things from you. You're your own keeper, and like seen within most facets of society, our actions can either mold and make a person, but also allow the necessary confidence for a person to exist without the thought or actions of a bully. How many times were you told as a child, "If he hits you, hit him back"? A very liberal friend once told me, "If we adopted the philosophy of an eye for an eye, the world would be blind". My question would then be, "If I'm not going to be my brother's keeper, then who will be?" That same person ironically refused to fight back when set upon, got stabbed and severely beaten as a result of a bully.

So, as a thought and a preventive measure, if you're going to allow and justify the very existence of a bully, know and accept he, or she, will not employ the same don't hit me and I won't hit your philosophy. Nor will they allow you to simply walk by and reserve the ill intended misplaced violence to be a one off. Their throw back, ignorant attitude and mindset isn't reserved for just a few, but only for those that won't hit back. I recently read that if you were to act in a passive role, welcoming a, "Ye olde mute witness" stance, you're not only blind, but as weak and cowardice as the bully themselves.

Jason Allday

Bunter Marks - THE T.B.F

"Being offended by someone's words more than someone's actions, says the type of person you are"- Anon

I grew up in Upton Park, St. Stephens Road. That for me was a good place, where I was surrounded by good people. Some were bad, but we went with what we had and made the best of everything.

We used to play at Plaster Park, which was our little bit of territory, it was government owned, but locally defended. We used to play football in the street, as there were a lot less cars back then, but those that did interrupt our game of football always got a kid's deserving mouthful of abuse. No one stopped or had issues, as we were kids doing and getting up to no real bother. We played on the local street corner, we kicked the ball against the wall, as much for the game, but if I'm honest, it was also to annoy the neighbours. We'd play knock down ginger for cheap thrills, but this was mischief and harmless fun for me. We would have a jigger (go-cart) made out of old pram wheels. This would of course turn modern day mum's hair grey, as there was no health and safety. We'd play kiss chase with the girls, NOT the boys, but each to their own. The over glamorisation and filth they put on the telly and push down kid's throats now a days is wrong! It was a place where every family knew each other. Saying that, we'd occasionally nick the milk off the doorsteps, but the milkman easily replaced it. Like most modern-day areas, it's all different now. So much has changed, much like most of the East End. Do I think it's the same? There are two types of working class, and what we see now isn't, and will never be a true representation of my kind of people. We had nothing, but there were rules. You understand and identify with that statement, or you don't!

My pals back then are the same pals to this day. Paul Harris, even though he's a Tottenham fan, and before you say anything, I agree, one's enough! Big Ted, all I can say is through thick and thin, that man is as high on my tree as anyone can get. Packi Singhy, admittedly there was no political correctness back then, but a solid and good friend who I've stood beside and against anyone. I have a lot of mates from Stratford and Leytonstone. They all know who they are; they are all good lads and were always there when it counted. If we were anywhere before a game, it typically was the Plough and Harrow pub. But at football, I was in the thick of it, placed religiously on what was once known as the North Bank, my spot and our gathering place.

A lot of the main crowd and faces at football know me as Bunter. It was a nickname earned from when I was very young and only a handful of trusted people know me by my first name. The irony is the other half were the arresting officers, but don't get me started on that one!

If someone was to ask me when I first started watching West Ham, and at what age, well, I didn't just watch West Ham, I went to West Ham... That relationship started around 1966 or '67. I'll add that there's no place for me in an armchair in front of the telly. There's a difference in a fan and a supporter! West Ham fans will give testament to this statement, 'anyone can be a fan, but can you be a supporter?'

Through thick 'n thin, I've been freezing my arse off on the terraces. I've been on and off coaches, beaten up old cars, trains, you name it. I've always been there and we always got there. The last thing we ever thought of was the planning on getting back. Getting there was more important. So, we went up and down the country, over land and fucking sea, by hook or by crook. I've had my fair share of rubber burgers and piss strength beer too. For me, dedication isn't a strong or an honest enough answer; there was a discipline and a commitment in what I did. It can't be explained, if you don't understand any of this, then the rest won't make any sense to you either.

I gained many friends from all different types of fans and from different teams. There's no other place for me on a social level that comes even close than the football crowd. It's funny, but I don't think I'd have the same type of mates than the ones I found at football. I mean, I can walk in a room, and get along with most people. It's not hard to pick up a conversation with anyone, that's the standard found with the likes of my mates. It's called respect and manners, the key ingredients to any healthy social existence. I'm glad I was involved in some great matches too. Whether we were watching, winning or losing, that's the West Ham way. This was put well by a younger lad when he said, "Being a West Ham fan is a promotion not a punishment, we acknowledge a loss and celebrate a win." So, for me being a West Ham fan is something I'm very proud of and that will never change. As for my reputation of getting up to some naughty things up and down the country, well that's another story.

Being part of a football community helped me to become a man. A Red blooded, claret and blue, football-loving, family man. I look back on certain events that occurred at football matches, some were of my own making and some by others, but at the end of the day it's all part of the parcel and the relationship you had with a 'football life'. You just can't have it all your way. When I'm asked by certain people on my past, I'm honest. I never blamed anyone for what I decided to do, as I'm a believer that you can't be a victim of your own decision-making. You are only a coward if you start making excuses for what you've been caught doing. Thinking back, I laugh when I got kicked by a police horse in 1965 outside East Ham town hall. I spent a week in hospital, and all I got was a scar, most of today's crowd would be calling themselves the general or the Guv'nor after such a minor event. I really should've put in a claim, but I doubt the police horse would've been brought in for questioning; but it might have paid for my season ticket!

What is that all defying important question on 'modern day football'? Things change, of course they do, that's a given. The world has become a smaller place with technology, but it's become an over saturated and commercialised one too. The identity we all gained at football is thinning away. Just recently, I was told of a fella from another country, snapping away with his camera in the club shop, all the while wearing another team's shirt! That is wrong on every level.

Christmas for some was a football and a new club shirt. It was one of the best presents you could get. There was a sense of pride and merit when you wore the same shirt as the team and club you stood by, whether a win or a loss. Your mum and dad had grafted for those presents, but it never broke the bank or left them penniless, you had a sense of ownership and gratitude and you'd be really showing off if you got the new club shirt, a football and a new pair of boots. Now that club shirt comes in different colours and styles. It's not a club shop anymore; it's a fucking boutique! My message to the 'industry' is keep it simple, and fuck off with your pandering to mass-market ideals and demands for a bigger bank account. The fans and supporters made the club; they're the anchors that can be found in all clubs and grounds across the country. Fans have supported the wins as much as the losses, not some over-seas Johnny looking for a kit for his stay at home poodle. Money allows a team and a club to survive, that's a given, but it has gotten out of hand. Look, I'll make my point easy and simple to understand. In the early years it was a much better game of football, not so many injured, one sub on the bench, a bucket of water and a sponge. We had one manager; there was one on the bench with the sub, but the football today, for fuck sake, where do I begin?

There's too many prancing about, shirts tucked in, with the personal stylists waiting in the changing rooms for the prima donnas. Part of the problem is the sickening amount of money involved. Good or bad performance, the players get paid enough cash to buy a small island. My opinion, no play, less pay. Now you've got 29 people sitting on the bench, plus too many foreign players, who are taking away the necessary building blocks of what's needed for a national team when the European or World Cup come around; not forgetting the inspiration that's being lost for home fans! What about the local lads trying to get their foot in the door? The teams that put up their players in any national game are there to simply promote their home teams with no regard for the winning or support of our national sport.

One major league player will go out and play against two or three of his club teammates that have gone home to represent their home countries for an international game. It's a total sham and embarrassing. Remember, it was working class people that built the support and following that made these clubs successful. Everything and everyone that came after this era are standing on a platform we built. The club is only big and successful because of us fans, not some poncy kid jumping like they're fucking Zebedee outside the grounds, thinking because they've gotten a new pair of trainers they've earned a voice and a right - fuck off, don't make me laugh.

See how those new shiny trainers help you when you've got some working-class northerner spitting nails at you and you'll come unstuck real quick. I'll touch in this subject lightly, as I feel it's important to pass the message on. For me and my lot, it was great in the day, but now you don't get no 'proper days', just skirmishes outside all the grounds, what was a test was being on foreign ground and territory. It was more than clothes with badges on the sleeves, it was more than a pair of imported trainers, and it was most definitely more than sitting at home giving it the large one behind a poxy fucking keyboard - it was about going on away games, trying to take their ends when paying on the turnstiles and defending your end at any cost. That was a buzz and a rite of passage!

The Teddy Bunter Firm name came about through a close friend of mine back in the early '70's. Another example of how mates were back then, you identified with the people around you and your stripes were earned, so to speak, by you sticking by your mates or your time and effort invested as a fan and supporter. Another was earned or awarded by way of your social gathering. It was a mutual pal named Simmo that should be credited to the making of the name, 'The Teddy Bunter Firm'. It all came about because Ted was the biggest man I knew, and being I was a regular fixture, one thing led to another and it all just fell into place. Myself, Teddy and of course a few good mates that never let any of us down were part of the group. Some might suggest that we adopted and kept the name, so to

Lessons

establish ourselves amongst the main firms, as there were a few groups forming at West Ham - Hornchurch, Cranham, the I.C.F, Canning Town and a few other groups. There were times we argued and quarreled amongst ourselves, but on the day, we all came together and formed a fucking handful for anyone coming down to our manor. My opinion was to make sure our efforts didn't go unnoticed; no man is an island as they say.

Now for all I've said, the principals I stand and live by and myself promoted morals, some may question a specific event I'm remembered for, certainly with a lot of the older crowd and mainstream press. It was late October or November 1977 I think, and after what was no different than any other football day; I met our little firm over at one of our regular pre-match pubs, if memory serves me right, it was the Queens head. Anyway, like normal, we set out for the ground ready for all and any that came down to give the cockneys a 'going at'. There were no incidents on the way to the ground, and surprisingly upon arrival to my usual standing place; there were none within the crowd inside either. That was until one person acted out on a subject I detest more than anything - bullying.

The person in question is a player that has been documented on to this day, as having confrontations on the pitch and around the game of football. By any standards, most football players have, being honest, been in another player's face, as football, like most sports can produce an emotionally charged situation that can test the most rational and calmest of people.

The two players that were part of the equation were one, who at the time was playing for Manchester City and the other West Ham. The West Ham player, who in my mind was a solid player who played and encapsulated what a team player was all about. He made the final pass for many of the goals scored by team mates, Tony Cottee and Frank McAvennie in the 1985-86 season, as this was a time when West Ham finished third in the First Division. A very humble player, who loved the game and played for all the right reasons.

The usual things were in play on the terraces that day, the banter, lads, fathers and sons, the songs and pushing and shoving, the real deal.

There was certainly no fucking popcorn, sitting down and gentle clapping. So, unbeknown to me, I was to become part of football terrace history. It was a good game, our side struggling then making efforts to get some lost soil back, you know, the old West Ham way, nothing easy! Like I said, I was standing down in my usual spot, when the visiting team's player, who in a shared opinion, made a questionable play and attack on the West Ham Player. I instantly saw red, I acted and without hesitation, my principals, morals and a firm member of the Teddy Bunter firm jumped over the barrier and set out to put this situation to rights. So here I am, I've gotten over the wall that was about the halfway line and confronted said poor player. Now by confronting, I mean with my fists and some verbal. I'm no judge or barrister, but my words were neither diplomatic nor befitting an audience with Her Royal Highness. In the mix, I received a flying kick from another visiting player on my calf. How many people can say they've experienced that during a live game? So, with what I thought was my point made and taken, I ran back into the chicken run where everyone was cheering, and as always, my firm were there for their own, they hid me from the old bill, allowing me to see the rest of the game and get home without any bother.

So, I'm home and safe as houses with my wife, Mal, getting ready for some tea and a sit down to watch Match of the Day, when who should appear larger than life on the telly, than yours truly! My first and only thought was fucking hell! Getting up the next day, the incident had largely passed from my thoughts until I was on the bus with Mal, and there I was again, this time in the Sunday papers. Not a big spread, but more of a mention. Again, I considered this no big deal, as all of the scuffles from the country's games were hitting the papers and this was not anything more in my mind, than my right to express my opinion towards a player, whose actions I didn't appreciate. The paper was folded in half, we enjoyed a lovely Sunday dinner around Mal's parents and another day had passed. Now this incident should've really been yesterday's news, but to my surprise, this wasn't going away quietly, as the Sun newspaper ran a bigger story with photos the following day in Monday's edition. So now I'm famous, The Sun newspaper had me bang to rights, claiming fame, not fortune in the high streets largest selling and read newspaper in the country. A few days later, the old bill were knocking on my door. Remember what I said earlier about neighbours, some good some bad? Well, there's a bad one - I hate grasses... that same neighbour always was a cunt!

So, I've been caught and like any decent person, if you do something by way of an illegal act or defined as a crime, you stand before the man and take it on the chin. So, I get the court date, and accepting I don't have a villa in the sun and a few million quid stashed away, I turn up. My Mal, who's as loyal as they come, also came to court with me. I think it was just to have a giggle at my expense and see me getting told off like a naughty schoolboy, but none the less, she was with me. I got a £200 fine, and if it wasn't for the fact Mal was pregnant with our first child, the Judge said the outcome could've been worse for me.

So, I stopped going for about a season, but like most things you value and have a passion for, you can't stay away for long. Inherently, we're a pack species, you need that comradery, and those friendships need to be maintained. Some would say that there's some that need looking out for in this harsh world, and equally as much, Saturday's isn't the same without the football and the boys. For me, football was where I found not only my 'feet', but where I came into my own.

Now to you, it may read or suggest that it was a simple case of a foul on the day. To me, it wasn't just a foul and it wasn't just about football. I personally had issues with players who intentionally played up, and regardless of the political climate and my mindset against visiting fans; this was about a player who was taking it too far. A lot of people have always said the same player was known for intentionally fouling players - as many have suggested, this was textbook bullying and someone throwing a tantrum. You've seen the scenario before, when someone takes his or her issues out on an undeserving person, and I simply wasn't having it. To think this was all the way back in October/ November 1977, and if asked today if I regret it, I would say, "Fuck no!" The fine and repercussions are another issue though.

What I did was wrong in some people's eyes, but it was correct and right in my mind and for the right reasons. There's no question of either hindsight or regrets, it was more than a question of right from wrong. It was a simple matter of my love for a game, and not accepting it being brought into disrepute through the misplaced actions of another player in front of me. To me, it's no different than if I'm standing in a pub or walking through a public place and I see a bigger person taking liberties with a smaller bloke. Knowing at least half of the story, I can guarantee anyone would step in and squash the bullying cretin. With bullying, why should anyone have to suffer because someone else has had mummy or daddy issues? If that's your problem, then why don't you join a gym or boxing hall! If you want to sort out your lack of self-esteem or insecurity problems, do it somewhere else and don't take it out on just anyone, especially on a platform and a place we call football.

Ok, I'm getting ahead of myself, so, yeah, he acted up and it wasn't the first time. I'm not a judge nor am I a jury. I'm a West Ham fan that despises a bully's bollocks attitude. What did you think I was going to do, write a letter to the board expressing my issues and concerns with what some may describe as a poor loser, who instead of playing like a pro, decided he'd play like a you know what! Anyone that knows me knows that my options were limited, but at least they were my own and I'll defend those actions to this day.

You see it everywhere in modern day society, and it is something most people have been a victim to, heard about or witnessed. One thing I won't stand idly by and allow is someone taking liberties with another person. I don't care what political party you lean towards, what your favourite colour is, I'm simply not going to stand by and let it happen, not in front of me. Like it or not, bullying is bullying, plain and simple! What makes this incident even more unacceptable is there's been so many players, who's actions are typical of childish like behaviour and this was not the first time a player had carried on like a child who didn't get his way. To add insult to injury, a professional player involved in the most watched sport in the world, who displays unsportsmanlike conduct like that, was really not ok in my book.... plus, it was against a West Ham player, so you know there'd be some biased objection from my point of view!

Could I be wrong? Yes, there's that chance. But as they say numbers don't lie and a leopard never changes its spots. I remember reading in early

2014, that a coach quit (or as some have suggested, sacked) due to an altercation and allegation that the coach hit a teenager, who was in an under 21's squad. It's up to you to investigate who it was and see what the accused persons name is!

I'll close this by saying, I pick my battles, I don't think I'm perfect, as I live in an imperfect world. What mistakes I've made in life, I live and stand by. I'd probably fail the litmus test on some subjects, but honesty, integrity and morals I'd pass with flying colours. Some people complain and are concerned with the cotton thread count of their imported bed sheets and that a local coffee shop doesn't have their favourite brand of crap-o-chino. However, they are the same ones that have the nerve to have comment on my actions.

Well my question to them, is what have you ever had the balls to stand up for in your life? I'd rather be known for something than nothing.

Jason Allday

Knowing what's right – Integrity above all!

Have you ever considered the complexity in decision making, that 'fight or flight', 'knowing right from wrong' – turning left or right? It can be agreed by many that regardless of the time and place, some things are probably constant – and that should always be the 'core' in your decision making …. Essentially your integrity. In the most testing or enjoyable of times (depending on your chosen/ preferred buzz), a person's inherent cognitive ability will contribute, to not only your principles but also your integrity – there should never be a question of what's deemed right – even when others disagree with you. A little-known fact about human nature – there's those that criticise and then do less themselves – glass houses.

So, what is the right thing to do? Your actions should stem from your deeply ingrained beliefs, a sense of discipline and loyalty – these should be a person's natural reflexes: In place at a moment's calling to protect yourself and those at your side and to defeat the wrongs while instilling the rights in a situation.

JEFF TURNER
WAR ON THE TERRACES

40 years ago, in October 1980 the Rejects released a double A side single, We Are The Firm/War On The Terraces. It ain't rocket science to see what influenced our band. Unlike all the other punk bands of that era, we were strongly into our ideal of punk being about running with the pack at football grounds and surrounding areas, living that life and transferring football hooligans into our gig venues. A rock n roll suicide? Didn't and don't give a shit! We talked the talk and walked the walk. The cover of the single was a photograph of West Ham supporters in the south bank trying to get at the Millwall supporters on October 7th, 1978. Very tasteful and homage to what was a memorable day. The first ever game I attended was West Ham v Chelsea on August 22nd, 1970. I was 6 years old; my ol' man took me and we stood in the packed lower west side. I couldn't see fuck all of the game if memory serves me right! The result was a 2-2 draw. West Ham were 2-0 up, but Keith Weller making his Chelsea debut after signing from Millwall, bagged a brace to secure a point. My outstanding memory from that game was not the result but the sheer ferocity of the supporters in the ground that day. A west side full of mainly Dockers, shouting, singing, using classic foul language and directing pure abuse at the Chelsea players and Weller especially for him being an ex-Millwall player. I was immediately hooked! My ol' man was fuming that the ex-Millwall slag had scored

against us, it affected him more than the Irons throwing away a 2-goal lead.

Being a nipper at the time, I couldn't understand why Weller was particularly singled out -because he played for that lot south of the Thames? I asked my ol' man as to why this was? My dad was a Docker; he explained to me that in 1926 a general strike was called for in the London docks, a majority being EastEnders and therefore mainly West Ham supporters who supported the strike and that the Millwall supporting Dockers south of the river refused to back them. Plus, Millwall originally being an east London club made him and virtually every other West Ham supporter naturally despise them. My ol man told me that in sept 1932, when he was aged 17, he went to Upton Park for what was the first football league meeting between the 2 clubs. He said the atmosphere was totally hostile, thousands of geezers in flat caps abusing each other and trying to get to one another and the filth trying hard to keep them apart! The scene was set for the bitter hatred between the two that exists to this very day. In December 1938, 42,200 punters packed into Upton Park for this fixture, a record crowd for a match between the 2 enemies that stands to this present time.

On May 6th, 1967 Manchester United visited Upton Park needing only a point to clinch the first division title (they caned us 6-1) their red army being arguably the first properly organised football firm in England. Hordes of the fuckers descended upon the Boleyn ground; they got there early doors and took the North Bank, our recognised 'End' at that time. It proper went off! West Ham came in and had a proper go, were game as fuck, but the Mancs tactic of getting in there early paid off. Just too many of them for the irons to take back the end. My eldest Brother Steve was there that day, he was 14 years old and has told me that it was a really heavy experience, real ultra-violence and West Ham were just unprepared but battled so gamely! From that day on they got with it. The liberty taken by the Mancs would never be forgotten or forgiven. Payback would come some years later, big style! From then on, West Ham mobilised and organised into a fearsome force. You would hear stories of the Mile End mob, the Boleyn firm, the Baker twins and if course the mighty TBF (Ted/ Bunter Firm). Upton Park became a fortress - 4 terraced sides in the ground, North Bank, South Bank, Lower

West Side and the Chicken Run; it was firmed up in every end; even rivalry's between different ends!

When I think about the late 60's, thoughts tend to be of the fucking flower power hippy brigade – I doubt if any of that lot were ever seen on a football terrace! The working-class youth never bought into that middle class, university peace and love bollocks and in late 1968, the skinhead culture was born. Booted, braced-up, stay pressed, clad boneheads were appearing at football grounds across the nation. The initial wave would only be a fleeting one. Come the early 70's there was a new look. If you watch the classic FA cup fourth round replay in 1972 between non-league Hereford and First division Newcastle when Hereford score their 2 goals (in a famous upset win) pitch invasions follow and it's a sea of gormless young-uns wearing fucking snorkel parkas! The music and films of that era were brilliant, but the fashion was shockingly turgid. The early to mid 70's oversaw a huge rise in football hooliganism. Fans were now kitted out in flared trousers, platform shoes, tank tops and sporting long hair. When watching footage of it kicking off in that time you notice the scarfs tied around their wrists and the older ones have sideburns, looking like they had just attended a Slade gig!

1975, the 25th October, Man-United came to Upton Park. West Ham were ready and in the mood to smash the 'red army'. The Mancs took a beating. Attacked in the south bank, they had to try and escape the battering they were taking, the only place they could go was onto the pitch. West Ham were after them from all sides of the ground. After 20 minutes of play being held up, they were herded back into the south bank and heavily protected by the ol' Bill for the remainder of the game. They took a pounding outside the ground too, a proper good hiding. I can vividly remember a back-page headline in one of the next day's Sunday papers titled, 'The defeat of the Red Army.' Revenge for 1967 was sweet and total!

As the mid to late 70's came around, I recall plenty of geezers on the terraces wearing Donkey jackets. For me that was a real menacing, working class, hard as fuck style. Very Ray Winstone in the movie Scum. The rise of punk had happened, but I can't recall seeing anybody wearing tartan bondage strides at the football. With the rise of 2 tone and the ultra-fake credential Sham 69, the skinheads were back on the terraces and in large numbers. In 1978/79 the Essex glory boy mods (mostly disenchanted ex-boneheads) were about in good numbers at Upton Park. Come 1980, style had become more casual. Harrington jackets, trainers, neat barney's etc. The early to mid 80's hooliganism and terrace battles increased sharply. It did become more about fashion; which totally baffled me and turned me off of the whole fucking shebang. Although the violence was heavy, I hated all the fashion bollocks, which has been my thing when it comes to slugging it out at the football. It became about wearing certain trainers, Pringle fucking jumpers and stupid fucking mullet hairstyles! When I went into battle, I never gave a fuck if my backup looked smart in his Lacoste polo shirt or Tacchini track top, just cared if he could throw a good right hand, have a core and stand his ground.

As the 80's came to its conclusion, the race scene was well up and running. Very soon the terraces would be a thing of the past, as all seated stadiums became compulsory. I still went and still go to the football but all low profile. Nowadays it just ain't the same as the good old days. I have been lucky to have experienced and lived through the golden terrace years and had the fantastic adrenaline rush of standing on them and rucking on them. Great memories' but all things have to end. Too many divs at football nowadays!

'It's all gone quiet over there. The seats and the stands are bare. Do you remember not long ago, all the times that we battled there -

WAR ON THE TERRACES. The Cockney Rejects.'
OCTOBER 1980

The murder of Rocky Dawson

Hit men, or contracted killing is a form of murder where a person or persons are hired to kill someone for monetary gain or profit. It's here that the difference between murder and killing needs to be defined. The most important distinction between a killing and murder is that of motivation and intent. A murder has the intent and is planned, whereas killing does not have intent. When the loss of life is accidental, the term used is killing. Loss of lives because of natural disaster and epidemic is also killing, soldiers kill, they do not murder in war.

Throughout history, there's been as many documented events that would warrant TV shows, books and films showing the premise, motive and events surrounding the killing or murder of someone or persons. In many cases there was a level of romanticism that typically condoned the actions, whether it be viewed as justified or condemned by the General public. Typically, the killing is associated with organised crime or a vendetta. Jealousy and other emotional traits are also tied to a contract. As much as we interpret the films as a source of great entertainment, it goes without saying that there is more than one victim from a gunman's bullet. Crime can be cold, but if you're ever to speak with a victims surviving family, nothing is more rigid or callus that a killer's motive to kill for money.

In Australia, between 1989 through 2002, the Australian institute of criminology conducted a study that showed of over 160 attempted or actual contract murders, the most common reason for murder-for-hire was insurance policies payouts. The study also found that the average payment for a "hit" was $15,000, and that the most commonly used weapons were firearms. Contract killings also make up a relatively similar percentage of all killings elsewhere. For example, in Scotland from 1993 to 2002, the percentage was slightly higher, accounting for 5% of killings and or murders. In the USA, Alabama is the #1 place in America to hire a hitman.

An employer, a hitman and a victim. The components of the mentioned area are as consistent as the very fabric and foundation of its structure. There's no other real credible consistency, other than its been reported in all four corners of the globe.

The crimes and events that hit main stream press are but the tip of the iceberg, taking into account current statistics that don't include the fact, or mention that government agencies around the world, have whole sectors and budgets dedicated to what is known on a larger scale, as espionage killings.

On May 2nd 2006, a stolen car parked outside a family's residence in Essex, with the contract killers inside, watched as the victim, Rocky Dawson, secured his 2 children in the vehicle. Shots were fired from the same stolen vehicle by one of the men, striking the 24-year-old in the back. These shots would claim the life of an innocent man and destroy a family. This murder you may expect to be reserved for Hollywood movies, not a leafy suburb in Essex, but murder was to occur and bring one of the darkest times to an innocent family, that to date still gives no reason or logic to the murder of Rocky Dawson. Rocky's surviving mum, Candy, took this harrowing experience as, it's not how you lose a part of your life but instead turned it into how you must live your life after.

Candy Dawson

"Love begins with a smile, grows with a kiss, and ends with a teardrop"- Anon

There's many ways I could describe the people that took my boy from me, the newspapers called them cold, ruthless callus killers, but no words will ever express my true hatred and anger towards them.

My Rocky was born on the 12th of April 1982, a healthy 10lb bundle of joy; I instantly fell in love with him. West Ham was a big part of our lives, so you can imagine our delight, as Rocky shared the same birthday as Bobby Moore. I named him Rocky after the films with Sylvester Stallone starring in them, some people were shocked when they heard this, but I always felt my Rocky was something special, a champion and a fighter, he shone in my eyes. I remember when his dad, Mark, was handed Rocky by the Dr.; I remember his facial expressions, him crying and the thought of a boy in the family. Rocky was the first grandchild in Mark's family. I remember how as a young boy, Rocky would go to his granddad's farm nearly every weekend, he was the apple of his granddad's eye, always full of energy and loved being around his family.

Rocky's childhood was like all the kids in the neighborhood, he had a lot of friends, regularly got up to mischief, and was really into his sports. He played football from about the age of four, up until he was about sixteen years old. I remember him playing for Havering district football team when he was 11, I was so proud of him. He also boxed for five stars for several years. Later on he would play golf with his dad and brother. He was always involved with sports, and got himself a job at a local pitch 'n putt while he was still at school, being around people was always part of his routine. Straight out of school, Rocky went to work. He liked his clothes and football, and to fund this, he knew he had to be able to earn. Season tickets and being the smart lad he was, wasn't cheap.

He had a good set of regular friends he would go to the pub or football with, never any real aggravation or trouble. He always put his family first, and thought the world of anyone in that circle. Even after moving in with his son and daughters mum, he would visit us regularly, I always knew my Rocky wasn't far away. I may be biased, and it's an age old saying from any mum about their own sons, but to me, my Rocky was the best son any mum could've wished for. He would always find time to talk to me, he was a brilliant dad, and his nieces thought the world of him; he was a large part of their lives growing up, he was more like a dad to them than an uncle. No one could speak badly of him. He was always happy and joyful around all the children; he was a big kid really.

On the 2nd of May 2006, everything changed; they killed not only my son, but took a part of me that can never be replaced. They turned my world upside down, inside out, they killed me inside too. Not only me, but also his children, his nieces, his family and every ounce of me was destroyed. I think about that day everyday, it's so cruel how the last day of my son's life was to be that way. Not a day goes by, or when I hear a siren I don't think of him. My life is cursed by a memory no mother should be left with, the last moments of my son's life, the last breaths he took and how he was murdered. I can close my eyes and still see the last time he smiled, the memory of him leaving the kitchen, his last actions and his parting comments. I remember Rocky got his children ready, he gave me a kiss goodbye, and walked out the door, this shouldn't have been any different from any other day but it was to be a day, that would cast a shadow over me forever. The only change in the routine was I'd normally see Rocky to the door and wave him off, for some reason I didn't. I know from the police report that he got the children safely in the car, all buckled up and made his way around to the driver's door, and that's when he was gunned down. I was still in my house tidying up when I heard someone scream, but I wasn't to know why. Still in my kitchen, I looked to see the door opening and my Rocky staggering into the room. It didn't make sense, I knew something was wrong, I asked him "what's wrong, Rocky?" The look on my boy's face is engraved in my memory. It's an expression I never thought I'd see, nor would wish upon any mother to see on their sons face. He said, "I've been shot" and collapsed in front of me. I remember screaming his name over and over again. My thoughts were not my boy, please not my boy. His nieces came into the room and were asking if he was ok? I just kept saying, "please God, don't take him from me"

The police and ambulance service arrived and asked us to please just step aside, I just wanted my Rocky to be ok. My son was lying on the floor in front of me, I was helpless, and I couldn't do anything. I didn't want to lose my boy. I remember watching Rocky being put into the back of the ambulance. I just kept saying again and again, "not my Rocky!" I couldn't lose my son. Rocky died in the ambulance at the scene. When I was told this, I wish I'd died with him. To hear his niece say how she would switch places with him, tells me how he was thought of by those that cared for him. They killed my boy, they shot him in front of his children, and they left a child to grow up only wishing he could share his life with his dad. When I'm asked, "where is daddy", all we can do is look up to the sky, point and say he's up there, and when his son asks what star, we simply say pick the brightest one and that's your daddy".

Two convictions were secured, getaway driver Christopher Pearman, 54, pleaded guilty to murder in 2007 and was jailed for life with a minimum of 23 years imprisonment. Hitman James Tomkins, 61, fled to Spain living under a false identity, but was tracked down to Puerto Banus, Spain in 2010. On April 1, 2011, Tomkins was convicted of murder at Woolwich Crown Court. He was later jailed for life with a minimum of 33 years behind bars before parole. It's been reported in mainstream media, that the investigating Detectives believe that Rocky Dawson was not the intended target of the gangland hit.

Jason Allday

He was gunned down in front of his two children, who were lucky to have not also been killed, my Rocky's life was unfairly cut short, and it hadn't really begun. I will never stop seeking justice for him. There are still people out there walking about freely and looking forward to a Christmas, a birthday and other celebrations with their own families, who were involved and know the reason why Rocky was shot dead in front of my grandchildren. I miss my son, my hero, my everything, my Rocky. I live with a level of anger and frustration that can't be truly measured or explained, but I also live with the children in my life. I will go on, I will never let my Rocky go. They took my son, but not my will to survive and contribute to the children in my family.

Quality, before equality

It was once written, that values can be considered the guidelines for living and our behavior. Typically, each person has a set of beliefs on how the world should be. For some, a culture, a peer group, or the society in which we live in largely dictates that set of beliefs. For others, it has been concluded through careful thought and often a reflection of experience, and is unique to each and every person. For most of us, it is probably a combination of the two. Values often concern the core issues of our lives: relationships, morality, gender and social roles, race, social class, and the organisation of our society.

Principles

Principles are the more logical, or moral, ethical truths, based upon our experience, knowledge, and values, on which we base our actions and thinking.

Moral and ethical principles are where a person's values come in. These principles grow out of deeply held beliefs and values, and are often the principles upon which we then reinvest back into those around us. Devotion to equity and fair distribution of resources, to a reasonable quality of life for everyone, to the sacredness of life, to the obligation of people to help one another – these all come not from logic or personal beliefs (which tend to be more biased) but instead from a value system that puts an emphasis on human dignity and valued relationships.

The same writing concluded, that treating everyone with respect and consideration doesn't mean you can't disagree with them, or even fight against what they're trying to do, as it's been proven, a healthy debate and conflict of ideals actually promotes rational thinking. Rather it means that you should approach them as equals and in some cases think they're actually right, rather than labeling or treating them as evil or idiotic. You're far more likely to get respect in return with that approach, as it's also been said, "If you listen, you might actually learn something". A very wise chap once said to me, "A closed book can only be shelved". To go a little further, one of the greatest ambassadors to the boxing world once said, "The service you do for others, is the rent you pay for your space here on earth".

Phil Dalby

"Its is easier to fight for one's principles than to live up to them"- Alfred Adler

Poland vs. England May 29th 1993

It was 7:30am, 26th May 1993, 35 Peterborough Ave, Cranham, Essex.

I was waiting anxiously, waiting for the sound of that diesel van to pull up outside my pad in Cranham, I knew the sound of that van like I know the intro to my favourite record, as I had travelled all over Europe in it. I had been in many sticky situations and many campsites with this truck. The sound of the horn beeping made me jump off the bed, and as I pulled the curtains and glanced through my diamond leaded light windows, I could see big Twichie with his window down smiling up at me and shouting, "Come on Dobsy we got some rubber to burn mate, and don't forget your passport and dosh!" - as if I'm going to forget these fucking important things.

As I grabbed my rucksack I heard the car door slam. Again, I looked out the window and I could see Tubbsy, who was out of the car with both hands leaning on top of the roof. Tubbsy was always a bit of a lady's man, with his shades on and a large smile from cheek to cheek, but all I could see were his two gold teeth shining up at me, all the while shouting, "For fuck sake Dobsy, hurry up! "Piss off, Tubbsy, you tart", was my reply.

Now if big twich' got out of the car and said that, I may have to swallow my words, as this man is the size of a walk-in wardrobe and loved his kick boxing, so you try not to fuck with him, but both were great pals, who have stood beside me in many hostile situations abroad and at home. I got my gear together and darted down the stairs, gave my girlfriend, at the time, a kiss on the lips and said, "see you soon, love". Now she was a lovely girl, a homely girl, and the girl that would do anything for you. My daughters loved her to bits. "Take care, Phil" she said "and try and stay out of aggro please". "Of course, babe, you know me" was my reply, and made my exit toward the van. My better half was standing in the doorway with a sad face, because she knew damn well what we are like when we all get together for these occasions. We took turns in driving the van, but this time it was my turn in the back of the van along with Twichie's and Tubbsy's bags and all the fishing gear. We always took the fishing gear away with us, and because I'm barred from any football ground in the world by the FA. We used this as a good cover and pretended we were just out on a fishing holiday, and we would always take the least unsuspecting border crossings so not to arouse suspicion. We pulled away and drove through Front Lane in Cranham, onto the A127 Southend Arterial road at the end of Front Lane, heading toward Romford, but took the first slip road on the Upminster Fly Over, so we could turn around and head in the opposite direction towards Brentwood. This is where we came to the Brentwood Roundabout, which brings us onto the M25 slip road, and so began our Journey on 'The Road to Hell'.

We were soon at Dover and had a few drinks on the ferry. When we disembarked, we changed drivers. Tubbsy took hold of the steering wheel, while Twich' had a lay down in the back and I was doing the map reading. It seemed like days before we hit the German border, and when we did we was greeted by someone that would never have won the personality award, not for any season.

Lessons

"Passport!" demanded the kraut customs officer who found it hard to crack a smile, like most fucking krauts. We passed him our documents and waited knowing they were going to spin us as soon as they looked at our passports, they always do! "Park ze car over there!" said miserable bollocks, and "get out of ze car now!" We parked up and got out...it was like a scene from escape from Colditz, all the police came running out with the sniffer dogs, and turned the van upside down. "I hope you're going to put it all back" said Tubbsy with that cheeky smile, "it took me fucking ages to pack, so you twats can mess it up".... that did make me laugh because they never understood a word he said. I could tell by Big Twich's facial expressions that he just wanted to punch them in the head, but thought better of it as he murmured some abuse at them from under his breath.

After an hour of being ransacked and bodily searched by the "SS" welcoming brigade, and I mean strip-searched and finding nothing, they decided we could carry on with our trip and allowed us to enter the shit republic of theirs. We had no intentions of staying in Germany, but after driving for hours and hours we finally arrived in Dresden and decided to call it a day, we booked into a cheap Hotel where we showered and got out on the piss.

Day two saw us arrive at the Czech Republic border, and into Prague, I took over the steering wheel, I found the Czech drive quite boring, just a single lane road and flatland, the views were nothing to write home about, so my mind drifted as we drove to the time we were all in Las Vegas, the Cranham, Rainham and Hornchurch boys. We had been out drinking at the Crazy Horse pub and we all wandered and ended up in a strip bar in the ghetto of Vegas. For fuck sake we had enough chemicals in our body to open up our own pharmacy. Inside this club it was pitch black with no windows and as we left it was daylight. We looked like the Lost Boys trudging through a dominantly black, bad arse part of the city. We stumbled across some locals, one who called himself 'Tennessee Tom' and his right-hand man who was called 'Sammy Sawn-Off'. Now you can guess why he was called that, as they started to show us their armoury and what drugs they can supply us with. At this point the rest of the homeboys came out and were very amused that we had got lost and were now on their turf. I told them all with Big Twich, Cliffy, Butch, Ray, Ian, Martin, John, standing beside me, that I thought they were a bunch of mugs, all waving their guns about, and that we were just like them. By that, I meant that all of us have struggled in life and if they wanted a fight, then fight with your fists and not guns. They replied, "You dudes look hard". I replied, "don't you worry about that Tennessee Tom, we will all stand here and fight 'till the end. You show me your gun and I will show you my fist," for some reason this gained their respect and so they started to show us their guns and let us hold them. I noticed a police helicopter hovering above us filming the whole scene. Tennessee Tom, who was obviously their main man said, "We like you dudes, if you need anything or get in any bother just tell people you know me," which was good of him, but I emphasized that I don't drop names in any situation.

With that, he wished us the best of luck and let us walk through his turf. We all shook hands, and carried on our walk. The rest of the chaps started walking. Butch, Ray and myself were last to leave and say our goodbyes, the rest of our boys were already quite a bit ahead of us so, as we trundled to catch up, I noticed a black man run out at the three of us with a machine gun. "What you doing on my turf, mother fuckers? You'll get shot" he said to us, I stood face to face with him and calmly said, "For fuck sake, mate you could have told us that before we walked down here, I would have stuck my bullet proof fucking vest on!" Butch and Ray stood right beside me as we waited for his response. "You are fucking crazy, man!" he said to me, "Yes I fucking am, mate" I replied and at that point I took out my pouch of tobacco and started to make a roll up. "What's that, mother fucker?" he said to me waving his machine gun around, I replied, "It's a roll up, mate, do you want one?" "Give me a roll up, mother fucker," he said to me and I immediately said, "Why don't you look in the fucking mirror, mate?" Now at that moment I was ready to try and make my move, but to our disbelief he started laughing. "Mother fuckers you are crazy, what you doing down here?" Butch said, "We've just been to see Tennessee Tom," "Mother fuckers, you know Tom, how you know Tom?", So I told him we met him and his firm ten minutes ago and he gave us his blessing to walk through this part of town. "Why did you not tell me you knew Tom?" he said, "I would not have bothered you". I replied "no worries mate, now do you want one of my smokes?". Laughing he replied "Ok, you crazy dudes, I will have a smoke with you, and you dudes can then carry on walking". At that point Big Twich, Cliffy, Duke, Dish, Johnny, Ian (pigeon), came walking back toward us, so he panicked and started to wave the machine gun about, "Who are these mother fuckers?". I grabbed his arms waving the gun and said, "calm down, pal, these are my mates and they are all safe, you have not got a problem ok". With that he calmed down, and smoked the roll up, we chatted with him and he let us carry on our walk back. That memory with The Rainham, Hornchurch, and Cranham boys will stay with us all forever, my mind now drifted back to the here and now as we approached the Polish border crossing.

Jason Allday

Tubbsy

We approached the Polish Border. Phil was behind the wheel, and it was here I was crapping my pants. Not because of Phil's known antics on our adventures, but because we'd picked up some weed in Dresden and I'd hidden it in the left-hand side wing mirror, and I was in the passenger seat. I had it in sealed bags wrapped around tight with cling film, so I deliberately put my hand over the mirror trying to stay calm. Two KGB looking officers in full leather trench coats and caps with the hammer and sickle imprinted in them met us at the border. "English?", was the greeting question. "Yes, mate!" I replied as they walked each side of us with one of them approaching me, the other round to Phil's window. "You all out the car now!" they shouted at us. "Take out your bags", what the next demand. Here we go, fucking spun again, I thought, but this time my arse cheeks were quivering at the thought of getting nicked and working hard labour in the salt mines in a communist country for fuck sake; and it was not a small bit of blow, this was enough to last the three of us a few weeks or more.

We all stayed calm and got the football out as they searched the van, trying to look not bothered as we kicked the ball around the border area. Our passports were taken from us and taken away. Tubbsy laughed and said, "I think it's Phil, whenever you're with him, we get spun. It can only be a result of special treatment or a bad omen". The border police came out and they crawled all over the Van, and thank fuck they never found our hash, it was a huge relief when one of the KGB looking officers came over to us with our passports in his hand and said "Go!". As we drove through we all looked at each other and let out a huge roar of laughter and started singing "Engerland... Engerland....! Engerland... Engerland......!, Engerland....!, Engerland......!" We were now on the road to Katowice and as we crossed the border, we approached the first town. The name escapes me, but I do remember all of the lorries in front of us were pulling over into the rest stops, as there were gangs of hookers in each lay by, all hanging through our windows offering sex, to be honest I was shitting myself. Me personally, I wanted something involving a lot less drama and less chance of a trip to a health clinic, so the obvious choice was to get our blow out of the wing mirror and respectively roll a huge Spliff.

Then from here we continued our journey. We found a little ranch style cafe on the main road, and by this time we all had the munchies, looked and felt totally wrecked. I took a look at the menu, but could not read a single word of it, the clear and obvious plus was everything on the menu was less than a pound, so we decided to order anything that sounded good, bit of a head fuck as we were changing from the Deutsche Mark into pure communism currency. All we wanted was a decent bit of food and now we're having to turn into Albert Einstein to sort out the currency rates. The menu didn't have any western sounding items at all, so we ordered a bottle of champagne and orange juice and nearly ate everything on that menu. The meal and champagne cost us hardly nothing so we gave the waiter a 5 Deutsch mark tip each, you should have seen his face light up, he started crying and gave us all a big hug and could not thank us enough. When you think of the situation, this poor fella was probably earning less than that a month, something even abroad I always respected was the working class. As we went outside someone was selling snide sunglasses at roughly £2 each, it was madness! We got back to the van and the roads were empty, only lorries on the road as petrol was so expensive, just empty roadways, and the roads were all ours as we made our way to Katowice.

Jason Allday

Phil Dalby
Football Hooliganism in Poland.

Hooliganism first developed as a recognised phenomenon in the 1970's and has continued since then, with numerous recognised hooligan firms popping up, with some large-scale brawls to boot (excuse the pun). Until 1997, the number of related incidents rose. According to Przemyslaw Piotrowski, of Jagiellonian University, the problem of hooliganism related to soccer and has been compared to what he has described as 'The Dark Days' of football hooliganism during the 1980's in Britain. Hooliganism in Poland is comparable in its scale to countries such as England. Many Polish clubs have hooligan firms associated with them, and there we were driving right into the heart of Katowice.

Mid-afternoon saw us arrive into the bustling town of Katowice and that mid-afternoon heat was thrashing down on our shoulders. I remember we all changed into our shorts and vests. One thing that rings true with us English, we appreciate a bit of sunshine.

Now we were on the prowl, searching for tickets for the game the next day, and as luck would have it, we bumped into two lads from Cranham, who both had packed in their mundane jobs and travelled all over Europe for a month on a budget of a tenner a day, traveling to watch the football and just using trains and buses as their only means of transport. They had informed us that we could buy tickets from the stadium, or so they had been told. So, we all headed in that direction with a beer in our hands, and a one skin Spliff in our mouth.

When we finally arrived at the stadium, what the lads had told us, thankfully was true, as the tickets were on sale for the mega price of what we worked out to be just a couple of pounds each! Un-fucking believable! We were well made up, so with that order of business taken care of we figured let's go and find a quiet little bar somewhere in the town centre and get smashed. We had been told that the night before there were hundreds of skinheads in Katowice on the prowl searching for the English fans, but we were ok, we found a nice bar with around 50 English fans that all seemed game.

The day passed without an incident, so we found a little bed and breakfast to rest our weary heads, but the only problem was that it only had one bed in each room; or so the owner said. We had to take it, but Big Twich was not happy and protested, "I'm not sleeping with any of you, I want the bed to myself" he said, following up with every other word being fuck this, fuck that! But that's Twich for you. He's a top man. We agreed to let him have the bed to himself, but wow, Tubbsy was not happy. "I can't fucking sleep in a bed with you, Dobsy" and "I'm sure as fuck I don't want to sleep with you Tubbsy", I replied. Now Tubbsy never lets anything get the better of him, so he decided to go on a midnight wander through the hotel, break into a room and drag back a single bed through the corridor, walk in the room and with that ever so confident smile of his and say, "See, seek and you shall find!" my thought was 'fucking top notch Stubbsy mate', as I was very much dreading sharing a bed with him. Knowing my luck, it would mean ending up with his legs all over me, thinking I'm a woman while he is in deep sleep or having a naughty dream. Eventually after a few joints we all crashed.

May 29th 1993, it's the day of the match, we all got up early and had some breakfast and hit the same bar we were in the day before. Rumours were going around about the polish skinheads again, as we sipped our beers in the early morning sunrise. "Fuck 'em, if they want it, we will give it to them", said big Twich. There was always the voice of reasoning that surrounded this giant of a man. "Too right!" added Tubbsy. Tubbsy then added, "We have been sitting in this pub in the square for hours now and everybody can see we are here, so where the fuck are these two bob skinheads?" Another English fan that overheard our conversation, which was one of the fifty or so who were drinking in the pub, then asked, "Ok to sit down with you?" "Yes, mate take a pew", said Big Twich, then he asked "What's the problem?", "No problem" Twich replied. The same fan added, "I have just been told there are over 250 English fans who have made a base in the Katowice Hotel, don't you think we should all head there, safety in numbers and all that crap. What do you think lads? Because if there are 300 skinheads out there and on the prowl, we will get the shit kicked out of us if they find us here". We could see this chap's backside was starting to fall out his pants. "Fuck 'em!" said Big Twich, "But I will go with the flow. What ever everyone else wants to do, I'm easy", "Me as well" said Tubbsy. The vote was unanimous; all the English fans in the bar agreed on the same thing and make our way to the Katowice Hotel. So, we made our way, slowly but surely. "Just follow the tram track heading East, it's about a 15-minute walk", said the lad.

Sure thing, the lad was right, as we approached the Katowice Hotel and crossing the tram-tracks that run right in the middle of the road, we could see a sea of Union Jack flags hanging everywhere, and around 300 English fans who made this Hotel the centre point. There's a sense of pride easily found, when you bring the greatest fan base in the world on an away game, to support the greatest sport ever played.

As we all mingled and got our drinks, I noticed some Chelsea fans handing in the Keys to a room to the hotel staff behind the reception desk. "Room 112, thank you, see you later, and enjoy your day". "Sure will", replied one of the Chelsea boys. Well I was just about to make their day worse. "Twich, Tubbsy, are you boys hungry?" "Fucking starving!" said big Twich and Tubbsy following up with a, "Why is that?" "I'll tell you why, I'm going to treat you, my good friends, to a slap up 5-star meal down in the restaurant". "Quality, Phil, top man", was the reply. "No worries" I said and with that we headed to the 5-star restaurant that was located downstairs in the Hotel. We all took a seat and immediately the waiter approached us and asked, "Room number please, sir?". "112", I replied. "Ok sir, help your selves to any of the food that is on offer, and enjoy your meal. Also, could you please sign your name and room number on here for me!" "Ok, no problem" I confidently replied, I took the pen and signed. Twickey and Tubbsy looked at me and started to piss themselves. "Fucking hurry up lads, let's eat like Kings then sprint like fucking Ben Johnson after this slap up meal from the Chelsea boys". We were laughing our bollocks off as we filled our plates to the brim and ordered Champagne to wash it down, we had tears rolling down our faces, and it was so hilarious. And when we finished the meal, we had desert, then sprinted out the hotel in a fit of giggles. As we ran up the stairs, we could see the hotel frontage. The atmosphere had changed, as across the other side of the tram lines were the Polish Skinheads, and in front of the tram lines were the Polish police, who were charging forward toward the England fans as bottles, bricks, stones and glasses came raining down on the English fans.

Out of the frying pan and into the fire, eh! I noticed the 2 lads we met earlier from Cranham at the front of the Hotel, along with the English fans who started throwing anything and everything back at the poles. As I turned and looked up, I could see televisions being thrown out the top floor windows of the Hotel by the English fans down onto the same police lines that were now storming the building. In fact, I even saw a single bed thrown down at them! The English fans then made a charge forward at the polish skinheads, while this was happening, a tram made the untimely mistake of passing through along the tramline. By the time it passed the two factions, there was not a single pane of glass left in it. It was destroyed from both sides; the poor passengers on board had to lie on the floor as they witnessed the total destruction of the tram that they were being carried on. You could hear screams faintly coming out of the tram, but these were overshadowed by the sounds of bricks and bottles smashing against the tram carriage. The fact that on this day, of all days, the Polish Government had disbanded, so it was left to police and army to govern and rule, and the only thing the un governed polish police were interested in, was arresting and beating up the English fans at the Hotel and leaving the poles alone and un challenged.

I witnessed a young lad and his girlfriend get beaten with truncheons to the ground. With this, I instantly saw red; I was not going to allow this to happen. The police, whatever their nationality or political standing were there to police and protect, not discriminate against innocent visiting fans. So, I picked up a huge wooden table and charged down the stairs towards the police, who were making the vicious attack on these two innocent people. I put all my strength into it and thrust into the police like an exocet missile that was out of control, sitting all three of them on their arses. I then threw the table on them as they were rolling down the stairs. I needed this like a knock on the door, as when you got ten or more things to do, anything extra is something extra you need to maintain, but I had made my move and now had to face the consequences. Anyone with a level of decency in them would've known this was the right thing to do. It is who I am, what's right is right and in this situation I'm not fucking wrong! At that point, another policeman ran up the stairs at me and attempted to spray me in the eyes with his CS gas that he'd pulled from his belt. If there is a lord, he must have been looking down at me, because this policeman never took into account which way the wind was blowing, and ended up spraying himself and walking round the steps like a blind man who had lost his dog. There is a god after all, I thought to myself laughing. The two lads could not believe what I'd just done. "Phil, come on, let's scarper, we need get out of here mate", said one of the young lads, but it was too late. As I walked down the stairs toward the old bill they decided to set their Alsatian dog onto me. Twichey and Tubbsy were wielding a chair, had stood either side of me as the dog started to sprint toward me. Now lucky for me, I was taught a trick at an early age. I grew up with dogs, so I had no fear of them and I'm not sure if it was Froggit or Terry that taught me this trick, but there's a method, that if timed perfectly, it can immobilise a dog. Now when necessary, I have done this with my staffs and my brother Paul's German Shepard and Doberman, both that are guard dogs and very vicious because that was the job and they had to be. But now it's for real and with a dog that I have no history with. As it bounded toward me, I could see its intentions and as it got closer I could see the eyes were focused solely on me, and when he was close enough, he jumped up at me and opened its jaws, I turned slightly sideways still trying to stay calm, and bulls eye, I put in motion the simple actions that rendered the dog incapacitated from inflicting any damage or injury to either myself or people around me.

Now I was in control, the Polish police were looking at me in total disbelief as I walked the dog down the stairs toward them. "Now call your dog off me, because I don't want to hurt it", I shouted out to them. As I continued to walk towards the police line with the police dog still under my control, I repeated my request "Call your fucking dog off me, or I will hurt it". Now for those of you that know me, know that I am an animal lover and I would never have hurt that dog, but I had to make the police know who was in control, and let them think differently. As I marched the dog toward them, balancing awkwardly on 2 legs, it begged me to let go of my grip. Beside me, Twichey and Tubbsy remained loyal and stayed, both still wielding chairs. Tubbsy said, "You've done it now Phil, but if you get nicked, then we all get nicked", Big Twich continued, "I second that!" I knew I was in the right here and assured them by saying, "Thanks chaps, but let's see what happens". At that point, as I marched the dog backward down the stairs the dog handler waved at me and whistled at the dog, "Shall I let go?" I shouted. "Yes, let go dog", he replied in broken English. I let my grip go on the dog, turned him toward his dog handler and he scurried off looking back at me. I'm guessing he was thinking to himself that should not have happened. To our amazement the police shouted to us, "You go, go now!" All the while in the background I could hear the sound of breaking glass coming from the Hotel. It was the jewelry window; it was a free for all by the English fans as they looted the shop. We were not going to hang around. In the mayhem and carnage young Martin had been arrested and beaten to pulp by the old bill, so we were lucky, for some reason we were left alone by the cops after the incidents. Young Stuart was lost without his mate Martin who had been nicked. This is where you step in, no question, so we took him under our protective wing and took good care of him as we headed toward the stadium.

    We entered the stadium probably no later than p.m., and you could feel the tension hanging in the air like a bad smell. We'd heard that one Polish lad was stabbed to death before the match, the Warsaw fans and Katowice fans had arranged a fight with each other and who ever won that fight were then allowed to fight the English. As we walked down the steps to the ground there was a wall about five feet high separating the poles from the English, the poles were running up to the wall throwing whatever they can at the English fans and spitting on us. This caused a chain reaction, the English fans then started to rip up the benches and steam back at the polish. Missiles were hurtling through the sky at a million to one, young children were being carried off on stretchers as rocks and bottles lit up the afternoon sunset, police and the army lost all control as the two countries battled to win the foothold on the terraces. British police were also on the pitch pointing out all the trouble spots. It was 45 minutes of total violence. The Polish police decided to make a charge at the fans starting from the bottom steps of the stadium, marching upwards and hitting out at any body that stood in front of them, even if they were innocent. At one point the police lost control and were run out of the top end tier of the stadium and were hit with lumps of wood, which was taken from the ripped up benches. I think you can still see this on YouTube if you type in Poland England 1993 Katowice.

For the first half of the game the police lost control, but then they come back with more men and firepower and eventually managed to get a foothold. The final score was Poland 1-England 1. After the game, we headed into town and picked up our van, and started to make our way to the next game, which was in Norway. Young Stuart met up with Martin, who thankfully was finally allowed out of Jail and they continued their journey to Norway by Train. We met up with them there and also met up with my brother Paul, Simon R, and Lou B for more adventures.

Thinking back, it's troubling to think how English fans are easy targets for foreign police. Admittedly they've a job to do, but they clearly didn't discriminate troublemakers from regular fans, as only English fans were targeted and were fair game! So, I will always stand up for what I believe in what's right, especially when pressed in a situation that questions right from wrong.

My chapter ends, but I knew we were in for more adventures. Shall we add it all to experience and lessons learned? It's all in the day of a life of a West Ham football thicky? It's quite funny, I think, as that's what we called everyone in them days, a football thicky.

Lessons

Being part of something special, as every dog has its day.

     A film, an actor and the value they carry - and of course the importance of being Mr Scott Peden. There's a common belief, that a man who can walk amongst the lions of industry, yet keep his touch with the common man, is a credit to the industry and the making of his craft. The mainstream film industry, that was once a credit in servicing the general populace with its productions, has become a diluted mush of efforts. What was once termed as instant classics and a testament to exceptionally talented script writing and memorable achievements is now an industry that is largely engulfed in a surplus of cloned and replicated stories. With luck and a constant truth in British film standards, a few productions and actors have managed to raise their names and efforts above the regurgitated trollop, as its been said, "It's better to fight and show your effort than sit idly by and accomplish nothing".

     So where does Joe public go to for a level of valued entertainment, that he or she can appreciate? One of the most common outlets is film. The British film industry has released some of the worlds most iconic and memorable films and actors. It's true that the lion share of what exists can be found across the pond, but what has been produced and remains a credit to the British film industry, is what have been found within the shores of our very own island. There's a lot to be said on being 'king of the hill', I could say it's better to be a cult classic than a best seller.

Part of the success in British film production is major companies coming to the UK because they know we are the best place in the world to make films. Everything is made easy, the political environment is conducive, and there's a lot less 'red-tape'. A common quote within the industry is 'the UK has a lot less stepping stones' and 'there's less hoops to jump through'. Another quality found within the U.K, is the fact we boast some of the most culturally diverse cities in the world, thus allowing a casting directors dream for the wealth of talent that may be needed and found.

An actor is as important as the production of the film itself. While some actors may carry the headlines, there are others that shine through and add both depth and value to the finished product. One-liners and symbolic statuses are earned as a result of a person's skilled craft and effort, and It's such personal investments that are seen with young British actors in classic films, that we are entrusted to value. Some would say, it's nice when the subject matter allows people to identify a precarious balance between totalitarian imperialism and an Independent thinking person, who hasn't been subjected to a political agenda! New comers like Ray Burdis, and Ricky Harnett are a compliment to the young, gifted and British. A belief by some people's perception is that there's a moral equivalence found in some industries, but thankfully not a shared talent in film and acting.

Actors can exemplify and carry a person's legacy - Scott is one such person. With his unique natural character, he allows both the watcher and the casting director to be challenged in fitting him in, and what better way is there than to be a stand out, individualist amongst the crowd? After all, isn't acting and its fundamental purpose supposed to carry as much entertainment value as a lasting impression? The authenticity with Scott amongst others, isn't a sophisticated imperialist one, it's Scott simply being himself.

Lessons

From his humble beginnings in Scotland, Scott has carried his own memorable efforts and style, which gave us characters that have been remembered and should be appreciated spanning multi generations.

Jason Allday

Scott Peden

"I may disapprove of what you say, but I will defend to the death your right to say it" – Evelyn Beatrice Hall

I was born in Auchinairn road in Glasgow. My mother and father, Anne and Thomas, were born and bred in Springburn. It's a working class area in the North of the city. My Father was a heating engineer manager in the Middle East and he spent a lot of time abroad. My mother was a district nurse in Springburn and she worked in the local community visiting old folks and patients who required help. When I was about 3, we moved to Bishopbriggs, a rather affluent area not too far from Springburn. What I distinctly remember is the name; it was given to by those in the surrounding areas. It was known as spam valley, as apparently the mortgage payments were so high, that all the inhabitants could only afford to eat was Spam. I have been brought up with a working class outlook and It's something I am very proud of, ironically, I don't ever remember being given Spam for dinner!

My Father returned from working abroad when I was about five years old and purchased some Glasgow black taxis. He has always been a believer in 'work hard and ye shall prosper', and as they say, you 'don't get ahead sitting idly by'. My dad had drivers working for him, quite often he'd do a few shifts himself, and he'd never expect or ask anyone to do anything he wasn't prepared to do himself. From what I can remember, it was a licence to print money in those days and the stories wee Tam could tell you were hilariously funny. One time he picked up a man who began talking to his invisible friend in the back. My dad played along with the game until the destination was reached. The man wouldn't get out until his invisible friend got out also. So, my dad placated him by asking him to get out with the passenger standing on the pavement beside him. Cue a Strathclyde Policeman walking along to see my dad talking to the back of his empty taxi. It was at that point the Policeman asked, "Are you alright driver?" Hilarious!! Sometimes, what society would claim are the useless idiots can be the best form of freethinking and indiscriminate type of people. My mother continued as a district nurse up until a few years ago, that was until she finally retired. Another testament to the working class ilk - there's no reason you shouldn't work, you don't have to be the CEO or industry leader, but any contribution is better than nowt.

I have a brother and sister, but there's a ten-year age gap, which leads me to believe I may have been a surprise! My brother, Gordon, is now a photographer in London and is a very creative individual. My sister Fiona, is a maxi facial surgeon, she too is very creative. In fact, come to think of it, creativity runs in the family. I think there's truth in the statement 'success and accomplishment is there for those who create it'. My Grandfather also was a great artist and loved a singsong. My own father could hold a tune and was very competent at drawing. My brother had a love for music and art from a young age. I know he loved and valued music, as he would go bonkers when I used to go in his room and touch his records and record player! My sister was a fabulous artist and used to draw constantly, she also used to make clay busts of various family friends. It seemed creativity ran in the family, but I was the only one to take it further in the performing sense.

I have a great family, very loving and always encouraged me to follow my heart and do what makes me happy. I was blessed and to be honest, it's that blessing I've never taken for granted.

My Father is a great man, caring, loving and very intelligent, with kindness in abundance. He is also very streetwise. In fact, you would need to be up very early in the morning to get anything past old Tam. Even to this day, my parent's house is never empty with people coming and going to see him and ask for his advice. His great saying is, "I am not any smarter than you son, I have just lived longer". Closely followed by, "If you lie down with dogs, you will get up with fleas". I think being streetwise and having a kind heart is a great mix. I really have been blessed with a great father, a hero and a great role model, as all fathers should be. We still have disagreements to this day, but that's because we are both similar. I love him dearly and couldn't have asked for a better man to be my father, he is a shining example to me what a father and husband should be. My mother always said that with my father, she never needed to worry about a thing. My mother is an absolute gem, very kind and compassionate. She's not long retired but after years of caring for old people in the community, she now suffers with slight arthritis - the aches and pains conducive with lifting patients for years, have taken their toll on her, but she says she wouldn't have changed it for the world. Mum believes that was her task in life, she really is a very caring person and came from a generation of nursing where empathy, compassion and care is everything. She would give someone her last and is always there for me, I love you very much mum. Her words ring out in my ears daily, 'Hold The Dream'. It seems only like yesterday she would stand and do the ironing while I would sit and play the piano for her. Great parents, great siblings, great family, very fortunate. She is still a member of the theatre group I went to as a kid, the Fort Theatre in Bishopbriggs. She is there every week and still acts in all their shows. That's where I must get it from!

My school days were hilarious, but not for my parents or the teachers! In primary school I was apparently a mouthy little chap, but hilariously funny. Looking back, it was just an abundance of energy, which came out in the wrong way. My mother said I had the whole school in hysterics when I was about seven. During an assembly in the gym hall at Balmuildy Primary School, there was a biting incident between two boys. While the head teacher was reprimanding the two of them in front of the whole school, I stood up and said, "Sir, dogs get put down for that". I survived primary school without a suspension, then in high school that changed, oh my oh my! That's where the class clown element kicked in. I loved making people laugh, it was like a drug. I was never malicious or nasty; I was just full of daft nonsense. I was never a fighter, however, if pushed I could and my temper went. It was like a pressure cooker. I would rather make someone laugh than hurt or fight them. I was forever giving wise cracking retorts to the teachers, impersonating them and making silly voices and going into made up crazy characters. However, it got to the point where if something happened, I would get blamed for it, even if it wasn't me and was due to my notoriety, and no matter how much I protested, I got the blame. This eventually caused me to have a level of resentment towards the school and some of the teachers. I was told, and I knew in myself, that I had the intellectual capacity to excel, but I had this energy that led me down the proverbial road of class comedian! I was who I was, but at the time, like most young lads, I simply didn't know how I could channel this 'energy'. It's saddening to think that in this day and age, children are unfairly prescribed medications to cull this free and creative eagerness that makes a child unique. As a result of my 'energy', I was suspended numerous times. Some of the more memorable stories are as follows. One break time we went for a sly smoke at the back of the school. This was the end of the main building with the stairs and glass windows from top to bottom. Just as we finished our cigarettes, my arch nemesis, the assistant head, to whom I detested, appeared on the stairs. We ignored him but knew he was listening. So, I whispered to my pal, "Lets talk nonsense as if we are on drugs". Cue a ten-minute conversation about vivid colours, parrots and being wasted. Just as we were talking about the amazing rainbows and the happy Hippos, the mentioned teacher appeared and dragged us along to his office, where he grilled us for an hour about what we had taken, when we had taken nothing at all. Sometimes I think the adult mind loses and forgets the creativeness from their own childhood. Maybe that's why there are more happy children than adults, as it's often said "children don't have a care in the world". I also think some teachers forget they're teaching young minds, not bad or old ones.

One part of my childhood that I've often reflected upon, is a part I like to call the 'labeling' part of my youthful misadventures. After a few suspensions in first and second year of high school, I was referred to a psychologist. It seems they were at their wits end. Maybe I had a mental health issue? I was seen intermittently over a 4-month period in Gartnavel Hospital in Glasgow. I distinctly remember being in the adolescent unit with my parents before each meeting and session. I would hear aggressive conversations and screams from other areas in the unit and to be honest, I felt vulnerable and out of place. There were other teenagers who were clearly disturbed in the vicinity. Even at that young age, I could see from their demeanor that they were suffering from serious mental health issues. Their demeanor and disposition spoke volumes to me. I think as human beings, we have an inherent ability notice when fellow humans are not firing on all cylinders. Even at thirteen, I could say something wasn't quite right with those kids. One such memory, which is still very vivid to this day, is when a rather overweight boy about my age kept walking up and down the corridor, intermittently shouting and grunting and violently twitching. I remember thinking, 'What the fuck am I doing here?' To be honest, it was scary for a me as a thirteen year old. I am an adult now and my compassion is developed and extensive, so I feel for that lad and I hope he has found peace. But when I was a young boy, all I could think was, 'There is fuck all wrong with me, get me fucking out of here pronto'

We had these strange meetings with me, my mum and dad and the psychologists. There was a huge mirror on the back wall where the rest of the team would stand and observe the session. There is a strange part of me that would love to do that now, as I could have some fun with that! I would go into character and just talk nonsense and watch the mayhem and confusion unfold! I remember the senior psychologist. It was Dr who had a bald head and a big bushy beard, combined with a Dutch accent. He looked like the type of guy who would frequent a nudist beach in open toed sandals and hug trees in his spare time. You get the idea!

They would show me pictures and judge my response to them. As an adult, I think of the hilarious scene in 'Analyze this', where Robert De Niro's character just talks absolute nonsense in his response to the pictures shown to him by the Psychologist to antagonise and mock the experiment. I would happily do the same now. You see, there's the humour again! However, he was very caring, compassionate and a consummate professional and he probably helped the kids who were severely disturbed and needed help, so he's a good man in my eyes. After the four months of sessions, questions, mirrors, grunts, screams and of course the face your Father pulls (when you say something stupid or silly in a serious environment, but he can't bollock you right there and then), my reaction to countless pictures and answering countless questions, you know what? Nothing! They told my Mother and Father, there is nothing psychologically wrong with Scott; he is very intelligent and imaginative! You see, there are dangers of a childhood in an adult world that exist in every part and level of society.

It also got to the stage where my parents used to have heart attacks if I came home early from school. They assumed I had been suspended again, even if I had a free period or a half-day. One of the funniest moments I remember is when my uncle Jimmy accompanied my father and me to a meeting with a member of staff with regards to my most recent suspension. Uncle Jimmy came away with an absolute corker. "These people that are assessing Scott, when was the last time they were assessed?" I know I wasn't perfect and my antics were mild in comparison to some of the horrors you hear today in Schools the length and breadth of the country, but I wasn't a bad teenager, I was simply a teenager in a place full of potential creativeness and opportunity. I just had this energy, vivid imagination and different mode of thinking that wasn't really conducive with the School environment. School really should be a place that young minds should be treated as a fire, adding elements to increase their strength, not like an empty bucket that can only hold so much. I mean, adulthood starts to slow you down and restrict what was once 'dreams and ambitions', to 'can't be', or 'shouldn't be done!' But, thinking back on my behavior and knowing both the expectations and pressures laid on the teachers by the powers-at-be, I send my apologies to those same teachers if they were scarred by my antics. However, I do also recall some of them laughing as they dished out the draconian punishment, so it wasn't all bad!

As I write this, I have just remembered the time I scrawled a huge penis on the blackboard and rolled it round the back of the board. Cue the teacher rolling it back round half way through the lesson, to reveal a huge chalk penis in all its glory!! It was like this electric feeling inside that said, "You are going to get into trouble for this, but if the laughter is of gargantuan proportions, then it's worth it". I sometimes like to think, that invested effort on my part, resulting in a class film laugh, could've made all the difference in someone's day. There was also another situation, which nearly resulted in suspension. My self and a good friend, who is now Warrant Officer the British Army, were thrown out of a class for doing Michael Jackson impressions. Full dancing, hip thrusting, fingers flicks and moonwalks accompanied the singing. It all started when the teacher addressed the whole class by saying, "Do you remember". She didn't get the chance to finish her sentence, because I jumped up along with my pal and started singing the Michael Jackson song 'Do you remember the time', finishing her sentence with the song's lyrics, 'Do you remember, when we fell in love, you were young and innocent then'. This was combined with the flicks and hand gestures and kicks of Michael Jackson. The class erupted and was incandescent with hysterics and laughter. We were both put in the adjoining empty classroom with our work as punishment. After about 20 minutes in the other class, I noticed the teacher's big fur-coat hanging up, to which I put on and climbed on top of the table impersonating her. My pal was laughing deep with loud belly laughs at my performance, and guess who came in? Yes that's right, the teacher. It was off to the assistant heads office once again for me. I often thought it would be easier if I just reported there every morning and save myself the long walk of doom to their office. As I write this, I just face-timed him after writing about him. He was in Bahrain with the British Army and he is due to take his commission to the rank of Captain. We laughed at our memories and schooldays antics and I told him he was mentioned in this book. He put it best, "At School, you were always doing characters and voices. When I discovered you were an actor it made sense. You had found your vocation at school before you even knew what it was". My pal, a lovely big fella who made something of his life and is one of your own. As an ex specialised Infantryman, I know his lads will have a great leader above them.

I must have been suspended about six times from my 1st to my final year of high school. All for stuff that was to make people laugh, it was never malicious or nasty. My feelings and thoughts on this are the world can be a cruel master, but laughter can be a welcomed ally in many situations, after all, dealing with the mundane school routine and carrying on the way I did, allowed me to find a platform that I benefitted from years after. Thinking about the level of evil and pressures on children from an adult ran world, some children take to the evils of drugs, I took to comedy, I made a healthier choice don't you think!

It got to the stage where I couldn't wait to leave school, in fact the school let me have 2 months off in my final year, and just come in for my final 4th year exams as and when they were. I was never cheeky, aggressive or belligerent; I was just very energetic and had a big imagination. Further to this, I wasn't fly enough to not get caught. The latter was my downfall when I had actually done something. I was easily distracted and that's when the mischief started. As I said before, the buzz of making people laugh was like a drug. I recently got in touch with an old school friend, Ross and he has obviously seen that I am now an actor and musician. He said, "I thought you would go on to being a comedian, as you were brilliantly funny at school". I didn't do too bad however and managed to get decent grades, which enabled me to get in to college to study engineering.

    Outside of school, I was involved in amateur dramatics at The Fort Theatre in Bishopbriggs - I loved it! The energy and gregarious behaviour seemed to work in that environment. I think that's where I got my first taste of the arts, I was hooked. When I reached thirteen however, I found the Air Training Corps cadet force. I was hooked on that a little more and left the dramatics behind for a few years.

    Myself and a friend, joined at the same time and we were fascinated with it all. We had to ensure we had the latest camouflage gear, boots, webbing and looked the part. I think that environment was also a good outlet for our sense of adventure and energy. This brings me to a commendable statement I was recently told by a friend 'south of the border'. "As children, we require not only discipline but also a form of leadership. Those that can't be disciplined as children, then learn to be undisciplined adults". Some great times were had. It was responsible for my interest in joining the military, and I loved it. I was never one for roaming the streets. However, we had a great social life with the people in our cadets. House parties and a whole manner of madness at our disposal. Even though I stopped drinking when I was 30, because I realised I don't actually like it, my staple supplies for that time was ten fags and a bottle of Diamond White cider.

    The arts had always appealed to me from a young age, and as I said before, that world seemed to fit my energy and imaginative mind. I didn't know that all those things I had been naturally blessed with, namely accents, mimicking, impersonations and being very observant, could actually be extremely useful when channeled in the right direction in respect to acting. I think it is something that is inherently within you. When I started doing it, I didn't feel nervous or any sense of intrepidation whatsoever. It just made perfect sense to me and I was hooked. I just felt comfortable with it and immensely happy that I had found my calling. Some people spend their whole life without finding their calling, or not having the courage to follow it, but I found mine and it just made sense. I also loved the fact that you can portray individuals on screen that are so far removed from you, it is unbelievable. I also remember when I was a teenager watching films and thinking 'I would love to do that'. Unfortunately for some, I did start doing it. However, as you know the location wasn't a set, it was a high school and resulted in me thinking my name was changed to, 'YOU BOY!', as that's what I was referred to by most teachers', who were obviously somewhat irate at my Oscar winning nonsensical performances! I feel fortunate now though, as I have stuck with it and I am getting a minimal bit of appreciated success. It's a long haul this game and you are learning all the time. I think the formulae for success is, no matter how long it takes, keep working hard, follow your heart and gut, and never ever give up!

There were a number of reasons why I left the Forces. The first reason was that I had met a Glasgow girl when I was home on leave for Christmas in 1999. It was one of those truly, madly deeply, head over heels emotions. Before that, I was your archetypical young man in respect to women. However, when I met her, I knew she was my first love. I loved her heart and soul and couldn't picture being without her. In my eyes she was the most beautiful thing I had ever seen. Mr Cupid had me in his sights and I was shot in the head as soon as I saw her. I was hooked! This love combined with being miles from her made me considerably unhappy. It was around the same time that I realised I had changed in respect to my outlook of my occupation. I loved the military, but the doubts had began to creep in to my thoughts as soon as I had arrived at my new posting. My Sergeant took an instant dislike to me and it was a clash in personalities in its entirety. Now someone who has a higher rank than you can make things difficult for you and can easily hide behind the chain of command structure. I am sure you get the picture. It's something that is commonplace and perpetuated in all occupations - I detested him. I heard recently he is a Policeman, that thought is rather disconcerting. He would probably be the type of Policeman that takes delight in abusing his authority like he did with me. However, I hold him no ill will and have forgiven him. Throughout this time, I did a lot of soul searching and the only thing that was always there in my life was my girlfriend. This made my longing for home and a different way of life even stronger. I also realised that we change as we grow older; our aspirations change considerably and are largely different to that when we were even five years younger. Part of me was incredibly worried about being institutionalised into that way of life. I would look at men who had been in for ten years, slovenly walking to the mess hall on a Sunday at each meal sitting and it frightened me.

I became deeply unhappy inside; it resulted in me being very distant with my colleagues. I wouldn't mix with anyone out with work and I longed for home. I would go home at every opportunity to see my girlfriend. My love for her was so strong, that I remember getting the 12-midnight sleeper train to Glasgow from Euston that got into Glasgow at 7 am, just so I could be with her on her Birthday. I got the same train back that night at p.m., as I was going on exercise the next day. The things we do for love eh? I can tell you, I would have done anything. That's what you do when you love someone heart and soul.

This pressure and deep-rooted unhappiness unfortunately descended into depression. It scared me, as I had never encountered thoughts and feeling such as those. It's human nature to fear what we don't understand, and believe me I didn't have a clue why this dark and morose feeling was raging over me. I thought there was something wrong with me, and I must admit it was a very dark and traumatic time. I began to resent my environment and the military ethos in general. It was strange, because I loved it. I became even more distant from my colleagues and I must admit that I may not have come across as a nice person. They didn't know what was going on inside my head at that time, how could they? They only saw the effects of the depression that was deep rooted within me. To be honest, in such a male dominated environment I felt I would be perceived as weak if I admitted to what I was going through. I could barely comprehend what was occurring in my own thought process and emotions so how could they? It was a viscous circle.

I mustered up the courage to see my own Doctor at home. I was in her office for less than five minutes and I broke down emotionally. All that pent up hurt, fear and unhappiness was purged in seconds in a flood of tears. It was a relief. The Doctor Immediately diagnosed depression. I was signed off from work right there and then and put on a course of anti-depressants. It was a relief. I now knew the reason behind my unhappiness and I felt a little better. At least I wasn't going mad, as I had previously thought.

I had three months at home and I revelled in it. It was very tranquil and the environment I was in aided my recuperation. Being in the company of my family and girlfriend done me the world of good. However, the environment I was so unhappy with followed me from the south of England all the way to Glasgow in the form of a phone call.

A Sergeant from the Medical centre at base phoned enquiring as to what was wrong with me. Please bear in mind that this man wasn't a Doctor. He basically insinuated that I was lying with regards to my condition and he was very sarcastic in his tone and manner. I couldn't believe that someone would take Doctors professional diagnosis into question. I could muster up something eloquent and befitting as to how I felt, but my initial gut feeling was to tell him fuck right off! I refrained however and he got a call from my Doctor, to whom was very irate at her judgment being questioned. I had no further correspondence from Sergeant 'Knob-end' after that.

With a sense of trepidation, I reported for my first day back at work. It was strange, but I thought that I would just keep the head down, as I only had a few months until I left for good. Unfortunately some individuals took to making light of my depression. One night in my barrack block, there were three of my colleagues in the room opposite. I went into say hello. We had a short conversation, but there was an atmosphere. As I left, one of them made a joke and said, "Ooh you gonna' get all depressed again". Now, anyone who has suffered depression knows there is nothing remotely funny about it. I didn't find it funny then either and that's when the red mist came down. There was an exchange of heated words, then more taunts.

Lessons

Remember I said that I have a sort of pressure cooker inside earlier? Well the lid exploded right off the pot that night!

I was livid and had this anger and aggression that just burst into me. This instantly showed with the enlarging of my veins in my arms and legs, you can just imagine it, I still remember it; the Hulk had nothing on me! It was then that I went to a storeroom looking for something. I found it right there and then - a large wood axe. I picked it up and went to the room. I kicked open the door wielding the axe, and I was immediately greeted by their shocked faces. I told the guy who took delight in taunting me that if he ever fucked with me again I would kill him. I truly meant it.

I'm not proud of that type of behaviour and I would rather help someone than hurt them, but please don't confuse my kindness and sensitivity for weakness. It resulted in the so-called hard man going to the guardroom and reporting that he was threatened with an axe. So much for the hard man eh? First sign of trouble he becomes a grass. Cue two Military Policemen descending upon my room with their pistols drawn. I will never forget the words they uttered outside my room, namely, "Put down the axe", to which I immediately complied with. The aggression in me had passed and I believed I had made my point. I was then detained and taken to a waiting police car outside the barrack block by one Policeman, whilst the other one carried the axe at the end of the shaft in his thumb and forefinger, following behind. I was then taken to the guardroom to see the medical Officer.

It was a very strange conversation on the way through the roads of the camp, one that was ironic in respect to my predicament at that time. The Military Policeman asked me the reason for my outburst. I told him that I just couldn't wait to leave this place. He then asked me, "What are you going to do when you get out though?" My response? I said, "I want to be an actor". It's funny now, as how many people who have just had a 9 mm Browning high power pistol aimed at them, relinquished of a huge wood axe, handcuffed in bare feet, shorts and T-shirt and after that then say, "I want to be an Actor". The Medical Officer asked me why I had acted in such a manner and I told him I had been taunted in this nature since my return. I told him I had had enough, and just wanted to let them know in no uncertain terms to back off, or else! I know I have that pressure cooker inside me, which very rarely rears its head now. I know its there, but I have learned to control it and make sure my brain is engaged before I act. Sometimes it's better not give away to individuals what you are truly feeling, or thinking for that matter. I am sure anyone from Glasgow shall know the term 'Take on'. It's something that was very apt in the aforementioned situation.

I can also look back and forgive those individuals from that time. If we don't forgive people, the anger and quest for revenge is like a poison. However, it doesn't have any effect on those it is intended for, it sadly poisons you. How ridiculous it that? Letting individuals who are no longer in your life still have bearing on your future and happiness. Without sounding melodramatic, I have become very spiritual over the last few years, and I know Karma is effective and it has no time limit. I always think of another one of my Fathers sayings, which is relevant; 'You can never educate a mug' so why try and get yourself worked up over someone or something that will never listen nor change. You just ensure you have awareness for those people and act accordingly. Some might say the best revenge is living well. I would agree with the 'Some's' whoever they are and wherever they may be.

It was a strange feeling leaving those camp gates for the last time. It was a tinge of monumental sadness, but relief at the same time. A part of my life was over, but I knew it was time to move on. As I drove through those gates, my mind immediately regressed to the end of my basic training. At my passing out parade, we had drinks in the mess afterwards. All the course instructors had got me to stand in front of all the recruits and their respective parents and do impressions of them. It was somewhat strange and ironic that even at the start of my military career the performing was there, and here I was hoping to embark upon that very performing as another. I will always be immensely proud that I was in the armed forces. I had some amazing experiences, in fact some of the best times in my life whilst serving, meeting some amazing people and traveling the world.

I will always remember the military humour. It is dark and is of the gallows type. It has stayed with me to this day. You can guarantee, that when your life takes a turn for the worse you can make a joke of it. I know every serving and ex member of the Military reading this will concur. The job I used to do had never changed, but I had and it was time to move and start the next chapter of my life, and follow what was in my heart from a young age; as they say, "Per Ardua...."

I split up with my ex girlfriend exactly five years after leaving the military. It didn't end well, then again when things end there is rarely any happiness. To be fair, she did me a favour. She wanted a man who worked a normal nine to five and also to have her own family and children. Yes I wanted kids, but I truly felt I had to follow my heart and pursue a career in music and acting or I would resent her in my later years. I won't go into what occurred between us, because it would signify an absence of class and integrity on my part, but we both know what occurred. She is married now and has obtained the life she so wanted, so I hold no ill will towards her at all and I wish her well. After all, I loved her from the bottom of my heart once. The passing of time brings clarity and it had to happen. I have got my dream, to do what I always wanted to do, and for that I will always be truly grateful. If we hadn't have split, I wouldn't be where I am today. Namely following my heart and dreams.

So, I left the RAF Regiment after seven years, and to be honest, I did appreciate the places and faces that went along with the 'experience'. My playground, so to speak, included working in places such as Bosnia, Canada, Germany, Norway, France to name a few. When I left, I knew that the creative industry truly was my path, but didn't have a clue how to start. A lovely fellow called Perry Costello, who was an armorer and prop master, gave me a chance to accompany him onto sets and show actors how to operate firearms safely. My Military background was ideal for that role and I have to thank him, as he didn't know me from Adam and was always very kind to me. I was young, keen and hungry and he gave me his time, thanks Perry.

Around about the same time I was working with my cousin in a petrol station in doing the security. The nonsense raised its head again. Well, to be honest, it's always been there, and that environment was ideal for it. In some ways, I think I filled a void. Funny voices over the forecourt tannoy, impersonations, and a whole host of pranks. One of my memories was impersonating the guy who delivered the sandwiches. He looked like Colonel Sanders from KFC and was always moaning. He came in one night to deliver and was moaning as usual. Cue me appearing from the back in a cardigan, slacks, glasses and a white hair and beard made out of cotton wool. I started impersonating his mannerisms and voice - he lost it and walked out. I thought he was going to have a heart attack! The other prank that springs to mind, was the time I thought I might be responsible for the death of an old woman. I won't name her, but she worked in the same garage at the fast food counter. It was common knowledge that she liked a fly drink whilst working, but she would deny it. The thing that gave it away however, was her eyes. When she had taken a fly tipple, one of her eyes used to open and close like an old airport arrivals and departures board!

One night I brought a replica 9 mm blank firing pistol into the garage, for what should have been an epic prank and wind-up. The gun was perfectly legal and I used it for work (I did work at an outdoor centre teaching children military skills on a military themed fun day). I waited until she was putting the cookers and ovens on and approached her and asked her into the back shop. In a serious and somber tone, I told her that a renowned gang of criminals who held up petrol stations may come that evening and hold the place up. I told her that if the inevitable happens, she is to go immediately to the back shop and not come out till I have dealt with it. She went all wide-eyed and didn't believe me. Then the realization kicked in and she agreed to comply. I then told her that she wasn't to worry, as I had something that would see the thieves off. It was then I produced the pistol from under my jacket to show her. She absolutely freaked out, and made a noise that can only be described as an angry monkey. As she did so, she slid down the wall behind her and began hyperventilating and struggling to get a breath. I panicked and immediately got her a brown bag from the sandwich bar, to which she used to regulate her breathing. The commotion was heard by another employee, to whom was working that night, he entered the back shop to see me standing over a woman with a 9 mm pistol in my hand and a bag over her mouth! I felt really bad after that, but the woman saw the funny side. Come to think of it, so did the same employee that walked in on it all. Once she had calmed down, he said in a sarcastic tone, "You will be needing a wee drink after that, eh?". Just goes to show how a prank can go very wrong and I still feel bad about that to this day. Although, I didn't mean any harm, but I could have hurt that woman. I think it's fair to say, sometimes, you should pick your audience. Thank God she had a sense of humour and could see the funny side. A big thank you to the family for giving me that job when I left the forces, and for putting up with my nonsense and all the customer and fellow staff complaints they received.

At the same time I joined an extras agency, as I thought it would be a good way of learning how the industry works. I am glad I did that, as I learnt so much about how a set works and how it all pieces together. I also remember the actors who came over and spoke to you and gave you their time. That meant a lot and was an example to me on how there's well placed intentions in an industry that can be very unforgiving. To this day, I always make a point of chatting away to the extras and thanking them. It costs nothing and I remember the people who done that to me. I have seen some actors be total cunts and ignorant to extras and cast and crew alike, and in my opinion that's not on. Treat people how you want to be treated. In life, no matter what your role or stature, we are all the same and there for the common goal. To make it be the best it can be. I will not overlook the importance of training, namely a degree course in acting, as it is valuable training and sets out the key skills as a professional actor, but I do think some people just have the attributes inherently within and learn on the job. There is no right or wrong in my opinion. If you can do what it says on your tin, then that's it. I just kept going, working and believing and never gave up....

I never did any professional theatre work. I've done plenty of amateur theatre productions when I was with the Fort Theatre in Glasgow as a child and a teenager, but the medium of film has always appealed to me. As a singer/ songwriter and musician, I would say musical theatre is quite appealing to me. Then again, could you really see me in plimsolls with jazz hands? Yes, that's exactly what I thought!

I'm still learning in this adventure they call 'life'. I think I would have to say to not be hard on yourself, and remember you are in competition with no one but yourself. The entertainment industry isn't easy, nor is it a road to immediate success. It's a long road littered with pitfalls and rejection, but the acceptances along the way make all those rejections worth it. You learn firstly, about yourself and secondly, the industry. Everyday is a school day no matter how long you have been doing it. In my opinion, the most important thing is to have tenacity and belief in yourself. Just keep working hard, never ever give up and enjoy everything that comes your way, as you never know where those things could lead. There will be doubters who you will meet along the way, just disregard them and never lose sight of your goal. Sometimes we can get bogged down and distracted by others thoughts and views on what we are doing. That leads to stagnation and loss of momentum. Be a lone wolf, work hard and do your thing. Never ever give up. This next piece may sound extremely self indulgent, but it conveys the aforementioned adequately. The lyrics to one of my songs says it all really: 'One man's Horizons are always judged by lesser men's clouds'

There's a lot of drive and energy needed in most things I've invested my life in, parents are a necessary energy and important set of role models, but some poor soles aren't fortunate to have both, or in some cases neither. Like I said, I was blessed. I think it's important to have a role model, all be it not an essential part of life. Steve Buscemi, is a person I could say is a person I admire greatly. Not only for his acting, but also for who he is as a human being. He was an ex N.Y.C Firefighter, and when the tragic 9/11 events happened, he reported to his old Fire House, suited up and went out with them to respond. He also campaigns to this day for the rights of N.Y.C Firefighters. That really touched me. In fact, anyone who has done considerably well and has never lost sight of who he or she really is and where he or she is from. That's admirable in my opinion, and there's a known saying in Glasgow - 'Not forgetting your old arse'. It's really inspiring to see people who have worked exceptionally hard and gained monumental success, yet it hasn't changed them.

My career aspirations are to keep working hard and to do the best I can in everything that I do. I think that's a great outlook. In terms of other occupations, I am also a singer and a songwriter with two studio albums released. Every Dog Has Its Day in 2010, and The Complete and Utter Confidence of Ignorance in 2013. I have been very lucky to merge both mediums. The film based on Paul Ferris, The Wee Man, I played Joe Hanlon, as well as supplying a track for the soundtrack from my second album. I have also done various soundtrack work with my music, most recently supplying a track for an American Feature Film, The Drama Club. I have also got another soundtrack gig coming up in a film I have been cast in for 2017, called Break. It's directed by my good friend Michael Elkin, a London born and bred lad and above all and everything else, a lovely fella and very talented. If I had to do anything else, I would have to say something that helps others and gives back to communities. When I left the forces, I worked at an outdoor centre that worked with kids with behavioural problems. I loved that and it was very rewarding. It's amazing how those kids would respond if you spoke to them in their own language. You could get through to them and earn their respect. It was then that you could engage with them and offer your advice. I loved that, so yes, definitely something that helps others. I'd add to that by saying, children are very misunderstood and misdiagnosed. Too often pushed away as society's problems, when in fact it's the adults that caused the problem from the outset. I think sometimes it's easier to blame those that can't defend themselves.

I would say that my favourite role was playing a Black and Tan Soldier in The Wind that Shakes The Barley in 2004. It wasn't so much the role, but more working with Ken Loach. What an amazing man and director. As an actor, getting a role in one of his films is an accolade in my opinion. What made it very special was that it was one of my first main speaking roles and that meant a lot to me. So I must thank him and the casting director, Kahleen Crawford for giving me a chance. To audition for that man, and for him to think you were good enough meant a lot to me, it really did. What a great team he has working with him, and time and time again he produces amazing films with social messages. It was a very strange audition technique too. He gives you an improvised situation to go with and then rather than watch it, he turns his back. I would imagine, listening to the flow and realism of the dialogue. An amazing time for me and it was actually quite emotional. I remember my first day on set thinking, 'me, Scott Peden from Glasgow has finally got a wee turn'. I was also extremely proud when it won The Palme De Or at Cannes. Even though I only appeared in a few scenes, it meant a lot that something I was involved in done well. So

I am eternally grateful to Ken Loach, Kahleen Crawford and all at Sixteen Films.

I would say the other favourite role was playing Joe Hanlon in The Wee Man. I think the part had more resonance with me, as he was a Glasgow boy. It also had certain pressure with it. Joseph along with his friend Bobby Glover was sadly killed in real life. Joseph had family, who would see my work and that was quite unsettling for me, so I knew an accurate portrayal of him was needed. I was quite worried about that if I am honest. However, at the premier in Glasgow, his brother said I had done him proud, as did Paul Ferris, so I was happy with that. Much love to Joe, Bobby and their respective families. It was also nice to have one of my tracks in the soundtrack, so it was a double whammy. I must thank the director Ray Burdis for giving me that opportunity. I got to know him quite well on that shoot. A lovely man, who is very genuine and talented, thanks Ray.

Life can really give you all the source material you need. Don't think of an experience or episode that has passed go to waste. In terms of the Wind That Shakes The Barley, it was my time in the military that I could draw on for character realization. I also found that a lot of the black and tans were Glaswegian. There was also a lot of criminals languishing in prison for crimes such as rape, murder, violence, who were pardoned and recruited into the British Army for the specific task of going to Ireland. I remember being quite disgusted at that. I don't know if it's true, but I heard one of the senior Officers at that time resigned or threatened to, if those criminals were recruited into the Army. As an ex-military man, I can understand why. I could only take my time in the military and take it to the extreme. I remembered the corporals and Sergeants in training - they were terrifying. They would shout and ball and be very aggressive in their manner. I just took that to the extreme. It seemed to work and it was quite scary to have that feeling still residing within you when the cameras stopped. That's what Ken Loach wants though. It's such a great feeling to have a director who gives you your dialogue, but also lets you improvise. I suppose that transposes well on screen, giving the abundance realism that all his films have. In terms of portraying Joe, I am from Glasgow and you have a certain way of seeing the world when you have been brought up there. One of the main things you have in your arsenal is a quick witted humour; you'll never win every fight and being from a city known for its violence, sometimes you'll need something other than aggression to survive. From what I heard, Joe had a light heartedness and quick wittedness in abundance. I was also told I looked like him a little bit from people who knew him. Like me, he was apparently always up for a laugh, so that was another similarity. Like any inner city, you know people of varying classes and lifestyles. This also encompasses the underworld. It's not, nor shall ever be my world, but I treat people how they treat me. So I just remembered some of the traits and disposition of individuals from that world and implemented them into my interpretation. Like I say, I hope I done Joe and his family proud. That meant a lot to me.

I think it's all about finding your niche as an Actor and I believe I have found mine. Strong roles encompassing Ex Forces, Gangsters and the archetypical hard man roles seem to be what I excel at. That's not to say my range can't do anything out with this, far from it. I also believe that it works in your favour when you do, as when people see you doing a role that is so different and so far removed from your usual characters, it somehow has more depth to it. Bottom line, I am just happy to be working, that's what every actor wants, don't they? However, you have to believe in the role you are going for, as you can't do yourself or the character justice if you are just in it for the money.

The whole game is hard, like any creative industry, as there are no guarantees whatsoever. That's life to a tee. You get up in the morning, same time as the next person, catch the same bus, make the same efforts, sometimes more, and then to find out you've come in second or third. Is that fair? No, but then life is sometimes just that, in some regards it could be viewed by some as a race; after all, there's a start to it all, so there has to be a finish line. Not everyone will cross it at the same time. It's something you get used to, but that thought is always there at the back of your mind, 'will I win, or get second?' The entertainment industry may not be for others, but it is for me. I guess it is a test of how much you are really committed to your art. You have to just keep going and believing. I would say the other thing that springs to mind is the perception of other actors.

Some seem to take a sort of delight in the fact that fellow actors are not working, or getting a role. On the other end of the spectrum, they are doing well and that's seen as a threat. I believe there is enough meat in the pie for everyone to take a bite, so just encourage each other. One day you will be working, the next you won't. All actors sample that at times and it's just the way it is. Like I said before, you are not in competition with anyone but yourself.

In my chosen profession, I don't think you have any other responsibility than to bring your character to life, and make it believable whilst delivering a good performance. Again, drawing from the 'everyday', when your alarm clock goes off, and not to sound like a fortune teller, but I doubt everyone jumps out of bed with a 'yippee, it's 4 a.m., let's do this!'. So, you have to make the effort, it certainly improves your chances! If the character is violent, or ensconced within that lifestyle and its relevant to the story, then it must be shown. When my alarm clock goes off, there's a moral obligation bestowed upon me that I identify with - effort! In terms of any other responsibility, I don't believe you have one in respect to violence. We all live in the real world, and in the real world we have violence occurring in varying degrees and forms. So when films are made to recreate life in all its forms, violence is a part of that unfortunately. However, I do believe that some filmmakers put gratuitous violence in for effect and it's something that has enthralled audiences for years. It's that, 'I can't watch, but I need to watch' mentality. It's in us all I believe, whether we admit it or not, it's human nature. There are those that say it's a catalyst for individuals to go out and recreate the violence they have seen on screen. I can only say that the large majority of us are aware of socially acceptable behaviour and also what is not acceptable. So, if someone does something that recreates the violence they have observed, I believe it's something which is inherently within that individual and nothing to do with what they have seen... in my opinion. After all, I believe we all know the difference between right and wrong, true or false. I grew up in one of the most violent cities in the world, with the main ingredients being hardship and heart ache, I took a risk and followed art and humanity, I wouldn't let the working class, hard earned invested efforts in me by my parents go to waste as I was educated to appreciate being part of something special ... how about you?

Coming of age

Coming of age can be best described as a young person's transition from being a child to becoming an adult. The specific age, at which this transition takes place, changes with both opinions and experience. However, one contributing key factor that should be acknowledged, is the transition seen clearly in differing economic and geographical societies.

There is one constant that remains true – there is not any one experience the same as another. For some, the experience can be one of bombshells and bullshit, for others, it can be an easier ride. It was once said, "10% of the transition can affect 90% of your life". But like most things in our lives, we romanticise the facts and hold hands with history. Some may say this is a way of masking the pain experienced from childhood. Whatever the reasoning and justification of a person's story, it is life's way of humbling us through humiliation, and giving experience with invisible scars.

One of the first requirements in development, once a young person's cognitive ability has started to mature, is the need to fit in. Whether it is in a social group, wearing the right clothes, music or sports teams; all of these give confidence. There are in many a person's young mind the components needed, to be successful, and also to help separate them from their childhood to become a righteous, stronger, self sufficient young adult. However there can also be in the same person's mind, a vacuum that instinctively, they feel needs filling. A form of self-discovery that is the path yet to be travelled by many, and when it is the coming of age, will be one that some will recall, as being one of light or darkness as two common components.

Other common detrimental elements, which can also be found within this formation time in a young person's life, are the feelings of alienation and fear. These two factors are often masked and catered to by anger and violence.

Thomas Turgoose

"Never be afraid to try something new. Remember, amateurs built the ark, professionals built the titanic"- anon

Like most kids, I grew up thinking no further than each day's events and the amount of mischief I could get into. I didn't have a care in the world really. My life was as much as I could have wished for as a child, but as much of that 'Peter Pan' thinking I once had, it was, as I learned later on an equally destructive part of my life. Growing up and having a family, even if it was only for a short while, allowed me to initially see the wonders and security found within the stereotypical model family. Bills were paid; we had an occasional visit to the sea-side on the bus and a meal on the table every day. On top of all of that, I had a few mates to hang out with, so who could ask for more? My parents separated when I was still young and one of my brothers and me stayed with mum. My other two brothers went with dad. I don't think it was a 'choice' and neither did anyone of us decide that one parent was better than the other. It was a simple case of some will go in that direction and some will stay here. I like to think we all knew we were still family, just simply in different locations.

I remember growing up, moving around a lot, and I even lived in women's refuge centres. Some of my best mates and priceless experiences I had were with other children during this time. Age-old classic adventures like conkering, swimming in the local lake; they were just harmless kids games and adventures. Deep down, I know mum never liked what had become of the situation; and I would occasionally see the stress in her face. But she always did the best she could for all of children. She dated some real losers; one in particular was a total knob-head. My eldest brother was always fighting with him, on one occasion I saw this same knob-head go into mum. Mum was a bit of a hard nut, a good strong Grimsby girl, she never let any man get the better of her, but that's not anything I wanted to witness nor should any child growing up.

When you look and consider how lucky I was with the film, This Is England, it's pretty remarkable considering I wasn't an actor nor did I even go to drama school. The casting director was looking for a child to fill the role, and of the millions of children in England, the tens of thousands of child actors, in a remote working class town not known for its block buster stars and films, it was here I was discovered. It really was a film that I had little interest in to begin with. I mean, at the time, I was simply Thomas, a child amongst three other brothers, who looked to be nothing more than the one who got the last word in and make people laugh. In layman's terms, I was a bit mouthy and took the piss when I felt I could get away with it. Even now, I find it pretty amazing considering the success and following the film gained. At the time, we all thought it would be some low grade, forgotten about film that no one would really pay much attention to. The memories of mum and her involvement, is something I remember well and treasure. She'd come along and watch every shot, she'd sit and witness her son being involved in the making of a film and she absolutely loved it. That is a comforting memory for me. I remember on one occasion, when we must have been about half way through shooting the film, the writer and director, Shane Meadows had some parts of the film put onto a DVD. He called a few people into his trailer to watch what had been shot and my mum was there. She cried through the entire time. There was never going to be another emotional time like that for my mum.

When mum passed, it was not long after the finishing of This Is England. We finished shooting in the September, mum passed that December. That flipped my world upside down. Like I said, for me it was something that's hard to process or get my head around. The day she died

Lessons

I still remember. It had been snowing a lot and I'd been out playing with all my mates. I went home as it was starting to get dark. I remember lying on the couch and falling asleep. Mum also lay on the couch facing the opposite end, the old top and tail routine. Two things I remember about that day. I had a wobbly tooth and mum accidentally kicked it out and my brother waking me up to tell me to call an ambulance. She'd gone up stairs to lay down leaving me on the couch. When the ambulance arrived, I didn't travel in the same ambulance, I didn't understand a lot of what was going on, but I know I didn't want to see her like that. My brother said to me not to go and see her, as she was in a bad way. Sitting at the hospital in the waiting room, I still had trouble putting things together. It was a very confusing, emotional and mixed up time for a 13 year old. It was here that mum passed away. The first people I called was Shane Meadows and Stephen Graham. Even before I put down the phone, both were in the car and on their way up to Grimsby. This was at 5.30 in the morning and by the time I reached my dad's place; both Stephen and Shane were there. They wanted to meet my dad as they had never met him and my welfare and safety was of the upmost concern.

Now here's something I'm not sure has been written about or said anywhere else, but it is a testament to the type of people I've learned to call my family, and that it the casts of both the film and the series I was originally in. It's a cliché term commonly said, but the two men mentioned are more than just family to me. There's something unknown about both Stephen Graham and Shane Meadows, and that is that upon hearing of the passing of my mum, they stepped up and offered to adopt me. By all accounts, I was very young at the time and neither of them was going to allow me to get lost in the system. They simply wouldn't allow any of those dangers to come my way. All of the cast are very special people and that can never be changed. How can you express your appreciation and put into words the respect you have for two people like Stephen and Shane? You simply can't! Both were willing to bring me into their families and raise me. No words can describe the love and admiration I have for those two men. There are simply no words that can I can say to express the emotion and thanks I have for them. What can you say to that? Nothing at all!

Jason Allday

Don't get me wrong, my dad was a good man and he raised me, but Shane and Stephen simply didn't know him. Dad raised me differently to my mum. There was a lot more discipline and structure with dad. I had gone from one end of the spectrum to the other, from a very care free life with mum to one of measures and strict rules. The rules and respect I had to show living with dad, was a necessary part of my young life. I only wish I'd spoken better to my mum. I wish I had shown her the respect I should've. When someone is gone, you can't apologise for speaking badly and mouthing off to them, that's one of my only pet-peeves with regard to how people speak disrespectfully to their parents. It's something you'll regret, something you'll have to live with, and something I know I'll have to live with. If I was to be asked how I dealt with that loss of my mum, I'd say it was with the implementation and necessary level of discipline instilled by my dad after mum died. That in many respects was a healthy and necessary level of structure. It was without a doubt one of the best things he could've given at that stage of my life. It would've been less healthy if I was left to mourn away in a room and not try and achieve something in my life. There was no more sitting up all night playing my Xbox, not bothering with school and generally getting away with whatever I wanted to do. I also think it was when I was sitting in the hospital waiting room, and hearing my mum had passed away, that I then decided that I no longer wanted to be the little shit that spoke badly to his mum, as this is what I'd become. I couldn't change how badly I'd spoken to or treated her, but I wanted to make a change and this was my opportunity.

Slowly but surely, I got back into socialising and that was thanks to my brothers. I met some great friends then, and that healthy change in my new social circle was a step in the right direction. Remember, I had come from having mates that were constantly in trouble with the police, to mates that simply went out, played football and never had any run-ins with the police. They had the same routine and structure I now had to conform to. Being in when they had to be, school every day and no major trouble. So it was definitely one of the best changes of scenery for me. These are the same people, that I'm still good mates with to this day. Probably within 6 months of moving in with my dad, he said he was taking us all on a family holiday. I'd never really been on holiday and as it happened, the film, This Is England, really took-off. Because we were in Turkey on holiday and I

Lessons

missed the premiere in Canada. However, shortly after we got back, my dad took me to the red carpet premiere in Rome. I'd never worn a pair of shoes, I'd never done my hair, never gotten dressed up and never walked a red carpet event. It really hit me when we got out of the chauffeur driven Mercedes at the event, stepping onto the red carpet and the hundreds of photographers, the thousands of people all there, it was then I asked myself, 'What the fuck is this all about?'. Don't get me wrong, it was a great feeling. I was a lot younger then and loved being the centre of attention. I was the class clown; I was the one who would stupidly smash a window so people would think I was cool. But this was a different kind of attention and for all the right reasons. I remember us getting a standing ovation, which must have lasted for at least 10 minutes. This was amazing when you think the film called 'This Is England', and the film was being shown in Italy and the crowd were all Italians showing such appreciation for a film culturally and geographically different to their own. I was buzzing. I had been acknowledged and getting attention for the first time for something achieved in a positive way.

During the filming of, 'This is '86', I was 18 years old and I was on cloud 9; when we were filming in and around Sheffield, there was all of the distractions you could imagine; girls, drink - all of it. I simply got carried away with it. After the filming stopped and the money was all gone (again!), I went to work in a fish factory! If life has a way of humbling you, this was certainly it! It made me think, 'I shouldn't be doing this', I mean I've had the perfect opportunities presented to me, with scripts, auditions and I lazily decided not to bother. I was passing opportunities up, and there were people that'd been waiting their whole professional careers to be given half the opportunities I'd been given. So yeah, it made me respect the chances I'd been given. Looking back I also know that experience of working a manual job, made me rethink a lot about myself, and if I'm being honest, with the opportunities that were sent my way that I selfishly and foolishly ignored, it made me grow up quite a bit. How can anyone say they're on the right track with regard to a career by going out on a Tuesday to drink, and not getting home until Friday? That's really not a way of investing in your success and it wasn't working for me.

Jason Allday

You'd think I'd learned my lesson after my initial success with 'This Is England!' I wasted all of that money, every bit of it. If I wasn't throwing it away on Chinese meals and what not for mates, I was buying and spending like there was no tomorrow. Part of the problem was there was no discipline at home. Don't get me wrong, I'm not blaming my mum. I remember she was very ill at the time, and passed away shortly after the film was released. There are no real regrets, and I think in my mum's heart and mind, she just wanted me to enjoy myself. She instilled in my brother and me that we could make it on our own, we didn't need a dad about. The fact remains my dad was there if we needed anything and was always there for us. In some people's mind, it could be considered my mum thought selfishly with regard to our well being, but that's water under the bridge - we all do things differently and no one is perfect.

One part of my young life that is deserving of mentioning is the youth program that allowed me to see the opportunities available. It was that same youth project that gave me the chance and opportunity, allowing me to see life's options. Well certainly a lot more than if I hadn't of gone. This was again quite remarkable, thinking about my success and gaining the lead role in the film. I never went to acting school and never had any thought or ambition to become an actor. The jobs and positions aren't always reserved for anyone person, I was a local kid growing up in Grimsby and got chosen for a film that reached millions of young minds. But an important thing to remember, which my dad reminded me of recently, as a person; you have to make that commitment and effort. Opportunities may and will present themselves to you, but it's your own effort and willingness to do so that will get you over the finish line. Someone recently said to me, "its 50% luck, and 50% effort". There were people there that made an impression on me at the 'Space Project'. So much so, I think of them to this day. It was their acts of kindness and genuine care that not only made a difference in my life but also to my late mum's life. When mum was really ill and struggling, they'd go out of their way and take my mum shopping. It's people like that, who will and should always be given a platform for their selfless acts. They asked for nothing and only wanted to help. These are very genuine people, grateful for what they have and identifying with the real needs of people in their care. I guess what you'd call working class heroes. There's truth in the saying, 'the more you put yourself into it, the more you'll get back'. A line my dad reminds me of frequently is, "don't expect to get anything back, that you didn't put in to begin with".

One very talented person I thought of just recently of was Amy Winehouse. She was such talent and such a loss. I honestly think the media played a role in her taking of her life. There was no forgiveness for any of her mistakes, mistakes that most people are guilty of, yet the mainstream media tore her to pieces. The poor girl couldn't as much as fart without it being front page news, and the dramatisation and embellishing of her private life was given no quarter. There was no room for error for this talented human being, who brought such an appreciated form of entertainment to her fans and she paid for it with her life. She could never make a mistake without the whole world passing judgement on her. I mean, how many times have you heard a lie about yourself and gotten pissed off. Can you imagine having the views and opinions of millions of people repeating that same lie? That's enough to piss anyone off. A lot of people can't comprehend the amount of pressure and cruelty that's sparked and promoted by some of the press. Remember, that same lie and bullshit is never forgotten. It might not be carried in the same strength and publicity for long, but by the same measure, it's something that'll be always there and brought up whenever someone likes. No one is perfect, including me. You should be allowed to learn from your mistakes, not be pushed into a corner and it cost you your life as well as causing the pain and suffering your surviving family will be forced to experience. The taking of drugs and alcohol is one of the easiest ways of masking that pain and suffering; all men are of flesh as they say and it is sometimes seen an easy way out for some.

I believe everything happens in life for a reason. Sometimes it really stings that my mum was never being able to come down to London and see what I've accomplished. That she never was my work, my place and the strong people around me. That's life, it'll sometimes give you a hurdle, and it's something you have to learn to deal with. I've lost friends to all sorts of shit who were taken at an early age. Life will spin you around and learning how you deal with that has to be ultimately be your own decision. It's not easy and it's not going to be fair, but coming out from those experiences will and can be part of your growing to a bigger and better person. With all of the situations and curve balls I've been dealt, I have learned to use them drive forward and take them as a kind of example to learn from rather than be an excuse. Admittedly this is a little later than I'd liked on some occasions, but I've seen what life can offer you, and I'm not going to be stupid and foolish again in letting them pass by.

Life has always been a risk and a gamble. That's ultimately the truth and messed up thing about it. Life can and will test you. Don't give up, but accept life is meant to be. Life is hard, life and its lessons aren't necessarily set to make you fail, but are more about learning to prosper from its tests. No athlete have ever got first place as a result of not training or dedicating their time and effort to their particular discipline. Things that present themselves as a kick in the balls will at first hurt, but you have to learn from every experience, good or bad. You have to experience loss to understand or appreciate the gains in life. Losing my mum made me appreciate my dad more, it taught me to understand how I was a little gobby unappreciative little shit, because in my heart I know that route would have been not only been a lot less productive one for me, but ultimately a short lived one too.

I'd be lying to myself and to you if I said I'd been more successful as I once was. Where has anyone come out on top as a result of being less respectful, and making no effort? I didn't get the acting roles as a result of not reading the scripts and not turning up, it was the complete opposite. I can't change what I once was, but I can change how I am now. Jumping over back-gardens to nick a bit of clothing off a clothes line was a laugh for a while, but there will be a time in life when not only the favoured bit of clothing but that type of behaviour also won't fit.